Eugene A. Maier

Dark Sky Rising

RECONSTRUCTION AND THE DAWN OF JIM CROW

By **Henry Louis Gates, Jr.**
with **Tonya Bolden**

SCHOLASTIC
FOCUS
NEW YORK

Dr. Henry Louis Gates, Jr.

In your hands

you are holding my book *Dark Sky Rising: Reconstruction and the Dawn of Jim Crow*, my very first venture in writing for young readers.

The book and its topic are very special to me for several reasons. When I was growing up in Piedmont, West Virginia, our American history lessons were mainly focused on the Founding Fathers and other great figures in American history, such as Abraham Lincoln and Theodore and Franklin Roosevelt. My teachers didn't dig deeply into the reasons for slavery, or why racial segregation happened. Back then, history class was all about dates and names, but not much about black people or the historical causes and effects of slavery and racism.

This is one of the reasons I became a professor of African and African American Studies.

Fortunately, I come from a family that loved to read and loved to discuss current events. My parents always taught me that knowledge brings meaning to one's daily life, and therefore to one's future. In fact, my mother and father often told my brother, Paul, and me that "knowledge is power." And so, when the chance came to write about one of the most turbulent and intriguing times in the shaping of America, I was very eager to present this important aspect of history to young readers.

The Reconstruction era remains one of the most pivotal yet least understood chapters in American history. Beginning with the Civil War and its aftermath, the United States struggled to heal the sectional divide that slavery and secession had caused while living up to the promise of equal citizenship for all, including the four million formerly enslaved African Americans who had played a decisive role in saving the Union and fighting for their own liberation. During Reconstruction, the Constitution was transformed. African Americans built businesses and religious and educational institutions, advanced an energetic form of government, held elective offices from the local to the federal level, organized and voted, and revitalized democracy itself against the longest of odds—and a constant, violent backlash.

Writing deep into the Jim Crow era that followed, the preeminent and pioneering black intellectual W. E. B. Du Bois wrote in his history *Black Reconstruction* that, during those transformative years of hope, struggle, and eventual betrayal, "the slave went free; stood a brief moment in the sun; then moved back again toward slavery."

I am fortunate to be collaborating with Tonya Bolden to bring the story of Reconstruction to students and families, who themselves are living through another period of urgency, consequence, and change. In cutting through the layers of false memories and other "lost causes," we seek to arrive at the heart of what Du Bois tried to teach us about the Civil War and Reconstruction, and the dreadful period that followed during the so-called Redemption of the South and the rise of Jim Crow segregation—the set of laws that enshrined "separate but equal" as the law of the land—so that you, a new generation of readers, can feel closer to your history and be vigilant about the complicated memory of Reconstruction, Redemption, and race in our own time.

Our book covers the half century from the ratification of the Thirteenth Amendment, which legally abolished slavery following the Civil War, and its fiftieth anniversary during the height of Jim Crow segregation. Our focus has been on presenting real-life accounts of resiliency and courage, creativity and uplift. Hopefully, this book will encourage you to ask questions about the legacy of the Civil War, to think deeply about history, and to develop some of your own ideas that you'll share as a participant in America's democratic experiment today.

Dr. Henry Louis Gates, Jr.
Director of the Hutchins Center
for African & African American Research,
Harvard University

Notable Awards
& Citations
DR. HENRY LOUIS GATES, JR.

Emmy Award Winner for Outstanding
Historical Program—Long Form, for
The African Americans: Many Rivers to Cross

PEABODY AWARD WINNER FOR *THE AFRICAN AMERICANS:
MANY RIVERS TO CROSS*

Featured among *Time* magazine's
"25 Most Influential Americans"

INCLUDED IN *EBONY* MAGAZINE'S
"100 MOST INFLUENTIAL BLACK AMERICANS"

Named a MacArthur Fellow

WINNER OF THREE NAACP IMAGE AWARDS

Selected as a National Humanities
Medalist

ELECTED TO THE AMERICAN ACADEMY OF ARTS AND LETTERS

Chosen as the National Endowment
for the Humanities Jefferson Lecturer

INDUCTED INTO THE SONS OF THE AMERICAN REVOLUTION

To Edward Austen Burke, Nathaniel Louis Gosdanian, and Ella Edith Parke Heinrich: May you live in a world in which racism is a historic memory.

Library of Congress Cataloging-in-Publication Data

Names: Gates, Henry Louis, Jr., author. | Bolden, Tonya, author.
Title: Dark sky rising : Reconstruction and the dawn of Jim Crow / Henry Louis Gates, Jr with Tonya Bolden.
Other titles: Reconstruction and the dawn of Jim Crow
Description: New York : Scholastic Focus, [2019] | Audience: Grades 4-6. | Audience: Ages 9-12.
Identifiers: LCCN 2018016732 | ISBN 9781338262049 (hardcover : alk. paper)
Subjects: LCSH: African Americans—History—1863-1877—Juvenile literature. | Reconstruction (U.S. history, 1865-1877)—Juvenile literature. | African Americans—Social conditions—19th century—Juvenile literature. | African Americans—Segregation—Southern States—History—Juvenile literature. | Southern States—Race relations—History—Juvenile literature.
Classification: LCC E185.2 .G37 2019 | DDC 973/.0496073—dc23

10 9 8 7 6 5 4 3 2 1   19 20 21 22 23

Printed in the U.S.A. 23
First edition, February 2019

Book design by Len Small

Table of Contents

1

Let Freedom Ring!

A sacred moment in a grove of live oaks draped in Spanish moss.

A song, impromptu, from the souls of black folk moved witnesses to tears.

My country 'tis of thee,
Sweet land of liberty,
Of thee I sing . . .

It began with an elderly man possessed of a strong, if gravelly, voice. Between one moment and the next, two women joined in. Soon more black voices were aloft singing of "rocks and rills," of "woods and templed hills," of freedom ringing out.

When white people lent their voices to the song, "I motioned them to silence," remembered Colonel Thomas Wentworth Higginson, remarking upon his tearfulness that day. "I never saw anything so electric,"

REACHING AND REJOICING: News of President Lincoln's Emancipation Proclamation, declaring freedom for people enslaved in Rebel-held territory, was cause for joyous celebration and for millions of black people to set their sights on a bright future.

he added, "it made all other words cheap; it seemed the choked voice of a race at last unloosed."

This electric, majestic moment happened on Thursday, January 1, 1863, more than six hundred bloody days into the Civil War, America's second revolution.

That grove of live oaks was next to Camp Saxton in Port Royal, South Carolina, which had been under Union occupation since late 1861. The gathering in the grove was a celebration of what the formidable Frederick Douglass called "the trump of jubilee": President Abraham Lincoln's grand Emancipation Proclamation. It declared people enslaved in Rebel-held territory *free*.

On the 1st of January, 1863, we held services for the purpose of listening to the reading of President Lincoln's proclamation.... It was a glorious day for us all, and we enjoyed every minute of it.

—Susie King Taylor, *Reminiscences of My Life in Camp with the 33d United States Colored Troops Late 1st S. C. Volunteers* (1902)

It was shortly after the reading of Lincoln's proclamation that the singing of "My Country 'Tis of Thee" swept over the vast crowd of thousands, roughly seven hundred of whom were members of a proud black regiment under Colonel Higginson's command: the 1st South Carolina Volunteers.

Land where my fathers died,
Land of the pilgrims' pride,
From ev'ry mountain side
Let freedom ring!

COMMANDER AND ABOLITIONIST: Colonel Thomas Wentworth Higginson's abolitionist activities included involvement with the Underground Railroad.

Dr. Seth Rogers, the regiment's white chief surgeon, also witnessed that moment of soaring song. When he wrote to his wife, Hannah, of "the most eventful day" of his life, he said that the "spontaneous outburst of love and loyalty to a country that has heretofore so terribly wronged these blacks, was the birth of a new hope in the honesty of her intention."

"Just think of it!—the first day [black people] had ever had a country," Colonel Higginson later proclaimed, declaring that "the life of the whole day was in those unknown people's song."

After Higginson addressed the crowd in that grove of live oaks, he presented the color bearers, Sergeant Prince Rivers and Corporal Robert Sutton, with the flags they were to keep flying high and out of enemy hands in battle. Prince Rivers vowed that he would *die* before he surrendered his flag.

Prince Rivers, a five-foot-ten dark-skinned man with light eyes, had endured some forty years in slavery on Henry Middleton Stuart's plantation along the Coosaw River near Beaufort, South Carolina, not far from Port Royal. A house servant and coachman, Rivers learned to read and write while enslaved. He did so at great peril. Rivers risked a brutal whipping, being sold farther south, or other forms of punishment if found out.

In early 1862, Rivers pulled off the ultimate act of resistance. He swiped one of his owner's finest horses and escaped from Edgefield, South Carolina, where Stuart had moved because of the war. Skirting Confederate troops, brave Prince Rivers rode more than a hundred miles to Union lines near Port Royal.

A born leader, Prince Rivers was not only a color bearer in the 1st South Carolina Volunteers but also the regiment's provost sergeant, its law-and-order man. Said Colonel Higginson of Rivers: "There is not a white officer in this regiment who has more administrative ability, or more absolute authority over the men . . . and if there should ever be a black monarchy in South Carolina, he will be its king."

"Contraband" is what the Union called Prince Rivers and other enslaved people who walked, ran, rowed, galloped, and swam to Union lines. "Contraband of war": confiscated enemy property used to aid the rebellion, from vessels and weapons to people. The designation began with the Union's General Benjamin Franklin Butler, a rotund and rather pompous man who hailed from Massachusetts.

Back on the night of Thursday, May 23, 1861, a month after the war broke out, three enslaved men—Frank Baker, Shepard Mallory, and James

Townsend—escaped from Norfolk, Virginia, where they were forced to do construction work for the Confederacy at Sewell's Point. Worse, they were soon to be carted off to North Carolina, separated from their families.

In a skiff and under cover of night, the three desperate men rowed across the waters of Hampton Roads to a fortress under Union control: the behemoth Fort Monroe, on the tip of the Virginia Peninsula. Baker, Mallory, and Townsend pleaded with General Benjamin Butler, the fort's commander, for sanctuary.

When the three men's owner, Confederate colonel Charles Mallory, got wind of their whereabouts, he dispatched an emissary, Major John Cary, to get his property back.

Since the start of the war, more often than not, when enslaved people sought asylum at a Union fort or camp, they were rebuffed—or worse, returned to their owners as required by the Constitution and the 1850 Fugitive Slave Act.

What would General Butler do?

He decided to keep the three men.

But wasn't Butler obligated to abide by the law? Major Cary pressed.

"I am under no constitutional obligations to a

foreign country, which Virginia now claims to be," replied Butler, a lawyer. He was keeping the men as "contraband of war." Virginia had used them against the Union. Butler would use them on the Union's behalf. Coincidentally, Virginia voters ratified their state's ordinance of secession on the very day the three black men escaped captivity.

General Butler would only reconsider his position if Colonel Mallory pledged allegiance to the United States. That didn't happen. Thus, Frank Baker, Shepard Mallory, and James Townsend were not hauled back into the hell of slavery. Instead, they became laborers at Fort Monroe.

Though I was a mere child during the preparation for the Civil War and during the war itself, I now recall the many late-at-night whispered discussions that I heard my mother and the other slaves on the plantation indulge in. These discussions showed that they understood the situation, and that they kept themselves informed of events by what was termed the "grape-vine" telegraph.

—Booker T. Washington, *Up from Slavery: An Autobiography* (1901)

SEEKING PROTECTION: *(Above)* Children and adults hung their hopes on Fort Monroe. *(Below)* People escaping slavery crossing the Rappahannock River in Virginia.

Word of General Benjamin Butler's stance spread fast. For black people in the area, Fort Monroe became "Freedom's Fortress." Within days of Butler's decision, nearly fifty had made a mad dash there. "Up to this time I have had come within my lines men and women with their children—entire families—each family belonging to the same owner," wrote Butler to a superior, General Winfield Scott, on May 27, 1861. Butler told Scott that he had decided to employ the able-bodied, "issuing proper food for the support of all, and charging against their services the expense of care and sustenance of the non-laborers."

African Americans were not only making tracks for Freedom's Fortress. "Within weeks" of Butler's decree, scholar Adam Goodheart tells us, enslaved people "were reported flocking to the Union lines just about anywhere there *were* Union lines."

In August 1861, the US Congress passed and President Lincoln signed the First Confiscation Act. It made General Butler's off-the-cuff decree law. By then, more than nine hundred black men and women, girls and boys, had made their way to Freedom's Fortress alone. One of those bold souls was Henry (Harry) Jarvis, an oysterman from Virginia's Eastern Shore.

Harry Jarvis was an imposing, impressive man. Over six feet tall and well built, he was said to have a "shapely head, a Roman nose, and the eye of a hawk" and "might have been a model for a Greek chisel—the young Hercules in bronze, or a gladiator ready for the imperial review." In the spring of 1861, Jarvis, twenty-five or thereabouts, made up his mind to escape after his owner—the "meanest man" on the Eastern Shore—shot at him.

For days, Harry Jarvis lay low in the woods with a friend bringing him food and news. Jarvis waited for just the right moment to take his liberty. It would come on the day of his owner's birthday bash, a time when the man and his friends would be boozing it up and carrying on into the wee hours—that was to be his freedom date.

Three weeks passed by the time Jarvis lit out in stolen goods: a canoe from a white man, a sail from a black man. After a stormy start, he was blessed with a steady breeze at his back. By morning, he was thirty-five miles away, across the James River and at Freedom's Fortress.

Like other black men, Jarvis yearned to fight for the Union. When he told General Butler of this desire, the white man snapped that it was *not* "a black man's war." Jarvis shot back that it "*would* be a black man's war before they got through." (Though black men, such as my fourth great grandfather John Redman, had fought for the nation's independence in the American Revolution, they were excluded from serving in the US Army in 1792. This wasn't the case with the navy.)

Instead of remaining at Fort Monroe, Jarvis joined the crew of a commercial vessel that would take him to Cuba; Haiti; and Liberia, West Africa.

Of course, back at Freedom's Fortress, Harry Jarvis's retort to General Butler was spot-on. For freedom was ringing out.

In August 1862, the Second Confiscation Act went into effect, rendering enslaved people who made it to Union lines "captives of war, [who would] be forever free of their servitude, and not again held as slaves." There was also a new militia act. It gave Lincoln the green light to employ blacks as laborers in the army for "ten dollars per month and one ration, three dollars of which monthly pay may be in clothing."

What's more, by the summer of 1862, slavery had been abolished in the District of Columbia and the western territories. The end of slavery in the capital came at a price that sickened abolitionists, though. The federal government was to pay owners up to $300 per enslaved person.

The two confiscation acts along with the new militia act culminated in the Emancipation Proclamation.

THE WAR BEGINS: Confederate soldiers fire cannons from an artillery battery, bombarding Fort Sumter in Charleston, South Carolina, beginning on April 12, 1861.

This 1863 decree, which Lincoln called "a fit and necessary war measure" for putting down the rebellion, fired up more black people to escape captivity. It also propelled black men, in the North and South, freeborn and freed—boatsmen, field hands, artisans, mechanics, merchants—to join the Union's armed forces, for Lincoln's proclamation also said that black men could be soldiers.

As fate would have it, the first black Union regiment came from South Carolina, the first of the eleven Southern states to secede (December 20, 1860) and the state where the war began when, on April 12, 1861, Confederate cannons blasted the Union's Fort Sumter in Charleston Harbor.

More than a year later, in late summer 1862, the Union's secretary of war, Edwin Stanton, an asthmatic and abrasive Ohioan with a beard, authorized the fiery-eyed yet gentle abolitionist General Rufus Saxton of Massachusetts, the Department of the South's military governor stationed in South Carolina, to raise black troops there. A few months later, Colonel Higginson was on the scene to take command. Thus, the birth of the 1st South Carolina Volunteers—or rather its rebirth.

Back in early May 1862, Union general David Hunter, then the commander of the Department of the South, declared people enslaved in Florida, Georgia, and South Carolina to be free. Hunter also began raising a black regiment in South Carolina. Prince Rivers was in that regiment. General Hunter had even taken Rivers on a recruiting mission to New York City, where some white people, livid over the sight of a black man in uniform, bombarded Rivers with stones and racial slurs.

Ten days after General Hunter issued his proclamation of liberation, Abraham Lincoln voided it.

At the time, the president was doing his utmost to keep the Border States from bolting. These were the slave states that had not joined the Confederacy: Delaware, Kentucky, Maryland, and Missouri. After Hunter's unauthorized actions, Lincoln tried to make a deal with representatives of the border states and Virginia's western counties, which had seceded from the "Old Dominion." He pleaded with them to agree to compensated gradual emancipation: payment for ending slavery at some point in the future. No, they said.

All along, Lincoln publicly proclaimed that the war was about the restoration of the Union, *not* ending slavery.

Then . . .

The winds of war, from the Union's failed Peninsula Campaign to take Richmond, Virginia, the second capital of the Confederacy, in the spring and summer of 1862, to the Union's need for more boots on the ground, caused Lincoln to change course. On September 22, 1862, five days after the Union's victory in the Battle of Antietam—the war's bloodiest single day of combat—Lincoln issued the Preliminary Emancipation Proclamation. In it, he gave the Confederacy one hundred days to cease hostilities. If it didn't, come January 1, 1863, he would release a final Emancipation Proclamation.

Lincoln kept his word, as the folks down in Port Royal learned when the New Year rolled around.

Decked out in blue jackets, scarlet pants, and broad-brimmed hats, Sergeant Prince Rivers and his comrades shouted "Hurrah!" throughout Camp Saxton on New Year's Day 1863. It was a day of surging jubilation, of freedom ringing out, of joy overflowing among liberty-loving people around the nation. In Port Royal, the day was capped with a grand barbecue!

The Road to War

The Civil War was a long time coming. Its causes include the following:

***Compromise of 1850 (September 1850)*:** This series of statutes was intended to defuse North-South tensions over the more than half-million square miles of land the United States gained for $15 million at the end of the Mexican-American War (1846–1848). This land included all or parts of present-day Arizona, California, Colorado, Nevada, New Mexico, Utah, and Wyoming. In this compromise, among other things, California entered the Union as a free state, slave trading in the District of Columbia (but not slavery itself) was abolished, and there was a new Fugitive Slave Act that favored slaveholders. For one, federal marshals in the North were compelled to assist slave hunters. Anyone abetting a fugitive could be fined a thousand dollars and imprisoned for six months.

Kansas-Nebraska Act *(May 30, 1854)*: This superseded part of the Missouri Compromise of 1820, which had admitted Maine into the Union as a free state and Missouri as a slave state, while banning slavery in the rest of the land acquired in the Louisiana Purchase (1803) above the parallel 36° 30'. This land included the territories of Kansas and Nebraska, where slavery would now be a matter of popular sovereignty, that is, left up to their white male settlers. This led to a violent clash between proslavery and antislavery activists, known as "Bleeding Kansas." The issue remained unresolved until Kansas was admitted to the Union as a free state in January 1861.

Dred Scott Decision *(March 6, 1857)*: Because their owner had them living on free soil for a while (in Wisconsin Territory for one), Dred Scott and his wife, Harriet, enslaved in St. Louis, Missouri, sued for their freedom and that of their two daughters. Dred Scott's case went all the way to the US Supreme Court, where, in his opinion for the Court, Chief Justice Roger Taney concluded Scott had no right to bring his suit, because, whether enslaved or free, blacks were not citizens of the United States.

John Brown's Raid *(October 16, 1859)*: White firebrand John Brown led a raid on the federal arsenal at Harpers Ferry, Virginia (now in West Virginia), with a small band of black and white men that included his sons. Brown's goal was to ignite an uprising among enslaved people in the area. The raid failed and John Brown was hanged. Thomas Wentworth Higginson was one of the raid's financial backers.

Lincoln's Election to the Presidency *(November 6, 1860)*: In the run-up to the election of 1860, many white Southerners, most of them Democrats, vowed "Dis-Union!" if the Republican candidate, Abraham Lincoln of Illinois, won the presidency. While not an abolitionist (an advocate for the immediate end of slavery throughout the nation), Lincoln opposed the expansion of slavery into the western territories. He wasn't alone. "Free soil" was one of the principles of the nascent Republican Party, founded in 1854. Some white Americans were free soilers because they despised slavery, others because they loathed the idea of wealthy Southern planters gobbling up the land. They wanted the territories populated by white farmers who cultivated their own small farms.

South Carolina's Secession *(December 20, 1860)*: At a convention in Charleston, the Palmetto State left the Union. It then urged others to join it "in forming a Confederacy of Slaveholding States." By the time Lincoln reached Washington, DC, for his inauguration (March 4, 1861), Alabama, Florida, Georgia, Louisiana, Mississippi, and Texas had heeded South Carolina's call. A month earlier, in February 1861, a new republic had been born: the Confederate States of America.

Attack on Fort Sumter *(April 12, 1861)*: Confederate cannons bombarded Union-held Fort Sumter in Charleston, South Carolina, until the fort's commander surrendered late the following day. President Lincoln promptly called for seventy-five thousand troops to crush the rebellion. Arkansas, North Carolina, Tennessee, and Virginia joined the Confederacy that spring.

2

Men of Color to Arms!

From the start of the war, like other abolitionists in and out of government, Frederick Douglass bellowed for President Lincoln to let black men fight in the US Army.

"The national edifice is on fire," Douglass fumed in the September 1861 issue of his newspaper, *Douglass' Monthly*. "Every man who can carry a bucket of water, or remove a brick is wanted; but those who have the care of the building, having a profound respect for the feeling of the national burglars who set the building on fire, are determined that the flames shall only be extinguished by [white hands]. . . . Such is the pride, the stupid prejudice and folly that rules the hour."

When black men were allowed to enlist, Douglass, based in Rochester, New York, leaped at the chance to serve as a recruiter. Two of his sons were among the first recruits. His oldest, Lewis, joined the first official black regiment raised in the North, the 54th Massachusetts Infantry. So did his youngest, Charles,

ACTIVIST, STATESMAN, NEWSPAPERMAN, AUTHOR: In 1838, at the age of twenty, Frederick Douglass, born into slavery on Maryland's Eastern Shore, escaped to the North, where he became a national leader of the abolitionist movement.

but he later transferred to the 5th Massachusetts Cavalry. (Middle son, Frederick, Jr., was a recruiter like his father.)

"Men of Color to Arms!" was Frederick Douglass's cry, as he traveled the North urging black men to rally around the Stars and Stripes.

To fight for God and country.

To fight for the liberation of their people.

To prove that African Americans—freeborn and freed alike—were fit for citizenship. To blast to smithereens the notion that, as Confederate president Jefferson Davis said, people of African descent were "a class of people not fit to govern themselves."

And fight black men did!

With bayonet, musket, and bowie knife. With their abilities at cooking, carpentry, blacksmithing, and piloting gunboats. With their might and muscle at digging trenches and digging graves. As drummer boys, chaplains, and physicians.

Black men (and boys) fought *hard*, and with valor.

They fought despite discrimination within the Union Army, where initially there were no black commissioned officers and black soldiers received less pay than white soldiers.

> **Now the main question is. Are we *Soldiers*, or are we LABOURERS. We are fully armed, and equipped, have done all the various Duties, pertaining to a Soldiers life, have conducted ourselves to the complete satisfaction of General Officers. . . . Why cant we have a Soldiers pay?**
>
> —Corporal James Henry Gooding, a freeborn member of the 54th Massachusetts in a September 28, 1863, letter to Abraham Lincoln

The Battle of Milliken's Bend, in Madison Parish, Louisiana, in June 1863 . . . The assault on Fort Wagner on South Carolina's Morris Island in July 1863 . . . The Battle of Fort Pillow near Memphis, Tennessee, in April 1864 . . . The Battle of Nashville, Tennessee, in December 1864 . . . The nine-month Siege of Petersburg, Virginia, June 9, 1864–March 25, 1865.

Black soldiers fought in minor battles, in major battles. And the bold Harry Jarvis was in that number. Yes! In the end he got his wish to be allowed to fight.

After nearly two years abroad, Jarvis returned to the US on a ship that docked at Boston Harbor in the

MEN OF COLOR

To Arms! To Arms!

NOW OR NEVER

This is our golden moment! The Government of the United States calls for every Able-bodied Colored Man to enter the Army for the

THREE YEARS' SERVICE!

AND JOIN IN FIGHTING THE

BATTLES OF LIBERTY AND THE UNION

A new era is open to us. For generations we have suffered under the horrors of slavery, outrage and wrong; our manhood has been denied, our citizenship blotted out, our souls seared and burned, our spirits cowed and crushed, and the hopes of the future of our race involved in doubt and darkness. But now our relations to the white race are changed. Now, therefore, is our most precious moment. Let us rush to arms!

FAIL NOW, & OUR RACE IS DOOMED

On this the soil of our birth. We must now awake, arise, or be forever fallen. If we value liberty, if we wish to be free in this land, if we love our country, if we love our families, our children, our home, we must strike now while the country calls; we must rise up in the dignity of our manhood, and show by our own right arms that we are worthy to be freemen. Our enemies have made the country believe that we are craven cowards, without soul, without manhood, without the spirit of soldiers. Shall we die with this stigma resting upon our graves? Shall we leave this inheritance of shame to our children? No! a thousand times No! We'LL DIE FREE! The alternative is upon us. Let us rather die freemen than live to be slaves. What is life without liberty? We say that we have manhood, now is the time to prove it. A nation or a people that cannot fight may be pitied, but cannot be respected. If we would be regarded men, if we would forever

SILENCE THE TONGUE OF CALUMNY

Of Prejudice and Hate, let us Rise Now and Fly to Arms! We have seen what

VALOR AND HEROISM

OUR BROTHERS DISPLAYED AT

PORT HUDSON AND MILLIKEN'S BEND,

Though they are just from the galling, poisoning grasp of Slavery, they have startled the World by the most exalted heroism. If they have proved themselves heroes, cannot WE PROVE OURSELVES MEN?

ARE FREEMEN LESS BRAVE THAN SLAVES

More than a Million White Men have left Comfortable Homes and joined the Armies of the Union to save their Country. Cannot we leave ours and swell the Hosts of the Union, to save our liberties, vindicate our manhood, and deserve well of our Country? Men of Color! all over the country, the Englishman, the Irishman, the Frenchman, the German, the American, have been called to assert their claim to freedom and a manly character, by an appeal to the sword. The day that has seen an enslaved race in arms has, in all history, seen their last trial. We are not free.

OUR LAST OPPORTUNITY HAS COME

If we are not lower in the scale of humanity than Englishmen, Irishmen, White Americans, and other Races, we can show it now.

MEN OF COLOR, BROTHERS AND FATHERS!

WE APPEAL TO YOU!

By all your concern for yourselves and your liberties, by all your regard for God and humanity, by all your desire for Citizenship and Equality before the law, by all your love for the Country, to stop at no subterfuge, listen to nothing that shall deter you from rallying for the Army. Come forward, and at once Enroll your Names for the Three Years' Service.

STRIKE NOW!

And you are henceforth and forever FREEMEN!

E. D. Bassett,	Rev. J. Underdue,	Frederick Douglass,	Rev. J. C. Gibbs,	Elijah J. Davis,	James Needham,	Daniel Colley,
Wm. Whipper,	John W. Price,	P. J. Armstrong,	Daniel George,	John P. Burr,	Rev. Elisha Weaver,	J. C. White, Jr.
D. D. Turner,	Augustus Dorsey,	J. W. Simpson,	Robert M. Adger,	Robert James,	Ebenezer Black,	Rev. J. P. Campbell,
Jas. McCrummell,	William D. Forten,	Rev. J. B. Trusty,	Henry M. Cropper,	O. V. Catto,	Rev. William T. Catto,	Rev. W. J. Alston,
A. S. Cassey,	Rev. Stephen Smith,	S. Morgan Smith,	Rev. J. A. Harris,	Thos. J. Dorsey,	Jesse B Gordon,	J. P. Johnson,
A. S. Green,	N. W. Depee,	William E. Gipson,	Rev. J. A. Williams,	I. D. Cliff,	Samuel Stewart,	Franklin Turner,
A. W. Page,	Dr. J. H. Wilson,	Rev. J. Boulden,	Rev. A. L. Stanford,	Jacob C. White,	David B. Bowser,	Jesse E Glasgow.
J. B. Seymour,	J. W. Cassey,	Rev. J. Asher,	Thomas J. Bowers,	Morris Hall,	Henry Minton,	

U. S. Steam-Power Book and Job Printing Establishment Ledger Buildings, Third and Chestnut Streets, Philadelphia.

CALL TO ARMS: A recruitment poster bearing Frederick Douglass's message urging black men to fight.

THE CHARGE: In the Battle of Fort Pillow, Confederate forces murdered Union soldiers in cold blood after they surrendered.

spring of 1863. By the end of the year, he enlisted in the 55th Massachusetts Infantry Regiment.

In late November 1864, Jarvis almost lost his life in battle in South Carolina. "There I was wounded three times; first in this arm, but I kept on fighting till a [musket] ball struck my [right] leg and I fell. I was struck once more in the same leg, and I lay on the field all night." Sadly, Jarvis lost that leg.

Along with Harry Jarvis and Prince Rivers, among the Union's gallant black men was Wyatt Outlaw, born into slavery in Alamance County, North Carolina. During the war, Wyatt Outlaw was pressed into service building Confederate fortifications near Petersburg, Virginia. He managed to escape and made his way to Freedom's Fortress. Outlaw then joined the 2nd Regiment US Colored Cavalry, which primarily saw action in Virginia.

There was also Robert Smalls, born into slavery in Beaufort, South Carolina. Early on in the war, Smalls was compelled to serve as head crewman of the *Planter*, a Confederate gunboat. But this man was far from content to do his master's bidding. He was ever on the lookout for a chance to escape.

In the early hours of May 13, 1862, with the *Planter*'s white officers ashore, twenty-three-year-old Smalls, dressed like a Rebel captain, deftly steered the steam-powered side-wheeler out of Charleston Harbor past several Confederate checkpoints and into Union waters. Six black crewmen were with Smalls when he commandeered the *Planter*. At the start of their perilous journey to freedom, Smalls stopped at a wharf to pick up his wife, their two children, and a few other family members and friends; seventeen people were on board when the *Planter* made its break for freedom.

When Smalls delivered the *Planter* to Union

OBERT SMALLS, CAPTAIN OF THE GUN-BOAT "PLANTER."

THE GUN-BOAT "PLANTER," RUN OUT OF CHARLESTON, S. C., BY

"PLANTER" AND
CAPTOR.

h an engraving of the steam-
ut of Charleston by her ne-

The following are the names of the black men who per-
formed this gallant and perilous service: Robert Smalls,
pilot; John Smalls and Alfred Gradine, engineers; Abraham Jackson, Gabriel Turno, William Morrison, Samuel
Chisholm, Abraham Allston, and David Jones. They
brought with them the wife and three children of the pilot,

by Captain Relay, of the Confederate navy—all the other
employés of the vessel, excepting the first and second
mates, being persons of color.
    Robert Smalls, with whom I had a brief interview at
General Benham's head-quarters this morning, is an intelligent negro, born in Charleston, and employed for many

on the following mo
sent from the city
contrabands were br
At about three o'clo
and the vessel stea
The tide was agains

HURRAH! HURRAH! HURRAH!: Robert Smalls plotted and pulled off a most daring escape in the spring of 1862.

officials, he handed them quite a prize: On board was a 24-pound howitzer and a 32-pound rifle gun among other weaponry, and a book of signals and codes. Robert Smalls went on to pilot vessels, including an ironclad, for both the US Navy and the US Army.

Christian Fleetwood was yet another black brave-heart in Union blue. Born free in Baltimore, this graduate of Pennsylvania's Ashmun Institute (today's Lincoln University) joined the 4th Regiment United States Colored Infantry at the age of twenty-three, and quickly rose to the rank of sergeant major. And Christian Fleetwood knew glory. In the September 29–30, 1864, Battle of New Market Heights, near Richmond, Virginia, Fleetwood rescued his regiment's flags after bullets felled both color bearers. "First night's sleep since 27th" he scribbled in his diary on September 30. Fleetwood and thirteen of his black comrades would receive the Medal of Honor for their valor at New Market Heights.

We are in winter quarters at City Point [Virginia] now, doing provost duty, which is quite agreeable after our Summer Campaign which has been quite severe on us at some

times. . . . I have a splendid little house to myself with a fireplace in it . . . . Only the recollection of home associations comes forcible to memory then I feel a little down hearted. But soon rally when I think on what principal [*sic*] I am fighting which is for the benefit of my race.

—Morgan W. Carter in a December 3, 1864, letter to a friend. Carter, a sergeant in the 28th United States Colored Infantry, was the son of Underground Railroad worker John Carter, a successful grocer in Madison, Indiana

Kendrick Allen . . . Solomon C. Banks . . . George William Commodore . . . George Dorsey . . . Toby Ellis . . . James Forge . . . Simon Grant . . . Henry Hancock . . . Albert Irvin . . . Zack Jaroy . . . Wesley King . . . Michael Leary . . . Octavius McFarland . . . the brothers John and Isaiah Owens . . . Spotswood Rice . . . Charles Stokes . . . James Monroe Trotter . . . Charles Vast . . . William Wright . . . Daniel T. Young . . . Charles Zimmons . . . and seven members of my family served in the US Colored Troops during the war.

When on April 9, 1865, Palm Sunday, near Appomattox Court House, Virginia, the Confederacy's top general, Robert E. Lee, surrendered the Army of

(Top right)
Sergeant Major Christian A. Fleetwood received the Congressional Medal of Honor *(top left)* for his heroism in defending the American flag.

(Bottom left)
A drummer boy named Taylor was a member of the 78th United States Colored Troops Infantry. He kept troops in lockstep with his percussion.

Northern Virginia to the US commander Ulysses S. Grant—the dawn of the Civil War's end—nearly 180,000 black men (more than half Southerners) had served in the Union's army (10 percent of the force) and 19,000 in its navy (20 percent of that force). Close to 40,000 died, three-quarters from disease.

Unheralded were the throngs of black people who had attached themselves to Union forces for freedom's sake. Men and women—children too—who had cooked for Union troops, cleaned, groomed horses, polished boots, did laundry, and served as teamsters, messengers, and guides for scouting parties and expeditions.

Company E, 4th Regiment United States Colored Infantry at Fort Lincoln in Washington, DC.

Many provided information about Confederate troop movements and other valuable intelligence.

If nothing else, in taking their liberty they deprived the Confederacy of their labor and sale price.

Also by war's end, three border states had come to see slavery as a lost cause and abolished it: Maryland on November 1, 1864; Missouri on January 11, 1865; and West Virginia (a state since June 20, 1863) on February 3, 1865. (The border states of Delaware and Kentucky stubbornly clung to slavery.)

After Appomattox . . .

After more than ten thousand skirmishes and major battles . . .

After the death of roughly three-quarters of a million Americans . . .

After the wounding of countless people in and out of uniform . . .

After areas of the South lay in wreck and ruin . . .

After nearly four million black men and women, girls and boys—about 10 percent of the nation's population, 90 percent of its black population, and about one-third of the South's inhabitants—were initially freed by flight, by legislation, and by a presidential proclamation, and ultimately by the Thirteenth Amendment to the Constitution.

After so many black souls across the years had been

slapped, kicked, bludgeoned, whipped, pummeled, paddled, raped, mutilated, branded, hamstrung, shot, stabbed, wrenched from family . . .

After more than two hundred years of stolen labor . . .

After all that, *What now?*

How would—how could—the nation heal, reunite, do right by the freed men and women?

OUT OF THE ASHES: Men and children posed against the ruins of Richmond, Virginia, the former Confederate capital.

Could the motto *E pluribus unum*—Latin for "out of many, one"—have a deeper meaning beyond the relationship between the states and the federal government?

Reconstruction, the process of remaking America, was underway.

Women Warriors

Elizabeth Bowser *(c. 1839–?)***:** Freed as a child by the wealthy Van Lew family of Richmond, Virginia, and later sent north to be educated, Elizabeth Bowser was a member of a spy ring organized by Elizabeth Van Lew. This Union loyalist got the young black woman work as a servant in the Confederate White House not far from the Van Lew mansion. In 1995, Bowser was inducted into the Military Intelligence Corps Hall of Fame for the valuable intelligence she gathered by listening to conversations, perusing documents, and by other means as she did domestic work. All the while, Bowser pretended to be slow-witted.

Charlotte Forten *(1837–1914)***:** This member of a prominent Philadelphia family was at the January 1, 1863, Emancipation Day celebration in Port Royal. She had arrived in the area months earlier to take part in the Port Royal Experiment: an effort to aid roughly ten thousand black people on the Union-occupied South Carolina Sea Islands who were living on cotton plantations abandoned by their owners. To prove that ex-slaves could function in freedom, Northerners like Forten went to the islands to help their inhabitants build schools and hospitals, and acquire other necessaries. In October 1862, Charlotte Forten arrived on St. Helena, home to fifty plantations. She taught at the island's Penn School, founded by white reformer Laura Towne. In the spring of 1864, the *Atlantic Monthly* published Forten's two-part article "Life on the Sea Islands."

Susie Baker King Taylor *(1848–1912)***:** At age fourteen Susie Baker was running a school for her people on Union-occupied St. Simons Island, Georgia. By day she taught children. By night adults. After she married her first husband, Sergeant Edward King, a member of the 1st South Carolina Volunteers (redesignated the 33rd US Colored Troops in 1864), she traveled with the regiment, serving as a laundress and nurse and teaching soldiers to read and write. Born into slavery on Georgia's Isle of Wight, at a young age Susie was

CHARLOTTE FORTEN: The journals she left behind are a wonderful resource when exploring Civil War–Reconstruction America.

LC-USZ62-7816

Harriet Tubman (1823-1913)
nurse, spy and scout

HARRIET TUBMAN was a mighty pioneer in the fight for freedom and equality. Though her exact birth date is not known, it is estimated that she lived past age ninety.

allowed to live with a grandmother in Savannah, where she attended clandestine schools. Not long after she was sent back to the Isle of Wight, Union forces took Fort Pulaski on nearby St. Simons. Along with other family members and neighbors, Baker made a beeline for St. Simons.

Harriet Tubman *(c. 1820–1913)*: This legendary Underground Railroad conductor served as a cook, spy, and scout for the 1st South Carolina Colored Infantry. In the spring of 1863, while working as a scout for the 2nd South Carolina Volunteers, Tubman engaged in intelligence gathering on Combahee Ferry, South Carolina, and environs—creating a spy ring along the way. What Tubman learned was critical to the regiment's successful raid of area rice plantations. It resulted in the liberation of roughly eight hundred black adults and children. Born Araminta Ross, Harriet Tubman was in her twenties when she escaped slavery in Dorchester, Maryland, in the fall of 1849. Her heroism before and during the war is truly remarkable, especially given the seizures she suffered, the result of a childhood head injury.

3

Fraught with Great Difficulty

"**I**, ABRAHAM LINCOLN, President of the United States, do proclaim, declare, and make known . . ."

This is from a wartime proclamation the president issued in December 1863, nearly a year after he issued the Emancipation Proclamation. Its title: a Proclamation of Amnesty and Reconstruction.

Rebels who accepted the end of slavery and swore allegiance to the Union would be pardoned, said Lincoln. Their property—except for human beings—restored. Exceptions included high-ranking Confederate officials, US senators and representatives who had joined the Confederacy, and Confederate soldiers who had abused black soldiers and their white officers.

With this proclamation came the president's Ten Percent Plan. If at least ten percent of a Confederate state's white men eligible to vote before the war accepted

PRESIDENTIAL PORTRAIT: Strong in his convictions, Abraham Lincoln gazes at the viewer.

his amnesty terms, that state could create a new state government and rejoin the Union.

Lincoln also announced that he would not object to "any provision which may be adopted by such state government in relation to the freed people of such state, which shall recognize and declare their permanent freedom, provide for their education, and which may yet be consistent as a temporary arrangement with their present condition as a laboring, landless, and homeless class."

The Ten Percent Plan got a thumbs-down from many of Lincoln's fellow Republicans in the US House of Representatives and US Senate. Especially galled were the Radical Republicans. These passionate abolitionists wanted the Rebels severely punished. What's more, they wanted not only true liberty but also true justice for black people.

They included the learned Massachusetts senator Charles Sumner, who had urged Lincoln to declare enslaved people free early on in the war. Sumner took the view that the Confederate states had committed suicide in leaving the Union and should be treated as territories, that is, ruled by Congress. The flinty Pennsylvania representative, Thaddeus Stevens, agreed.

There was also Ohio's Senator Benjamin Franklin Wade. In February 1864, Wade and another radical,

Maryland's Representative Henry Winter Davis, sponsored a bill with much tougher requirements for a former Confederate state to be readmitted to the Union. For one, a *majority* of its eligible voters had to swear allegiance to the Union. The Wade-Davis Bill also called for the president to appoint military governors for the states that had seceded. The bill cleared

THE "RAIL SPLITTER" AT WORK REPAIRING THE UNION.

A NATION DIVIDED: This political cartoon shows Vice President Andrew Johnson on top of a globe, trying to mend a map of the US. Abraham Lincoln supports the globe with a split rail.

Congress in July 1864. Lincoln responded to it with a "pocket veto," that is, he simply didn't sign it, just tucked it away, so to speak.

Earlier that spring, on April 8, 1864, the US Senate passed the Thirteenth Amendment to the US Constitution: "Neither slavery nor involuntary servitude, except as a punishment for crime whereof the party shall have been duly convicted, shall exist within the United States, or any place subject to their jurisdiction."

It took a while—nine months—but finally, on January 31, 1865, the amendment passed in the House. As mandated by the Constitution, the amendment was then sent to the states for ratification. It was ratified on December 6 of that year, finally abolishing slavery in the United States, eight months after the end of the Civil War.

On January 16, 1865, the Union's General William Tecumseh Sherman issued a field order that met with hearty support from black people and their white allies. The irascible Sherman had recently completed his March to the Sea, inflicting about $100 million worth of damage on Georgia between the time that his more than sixty thousand troops left Atlanta in mid-November 1864 and reached Savannah on December 21, 1864. Thousands of black people made their great escape with that army. A few weeks after Sherman captured

Savannah, his "Christmas gift" to Lincoln, he issued Special Field Order No. 15.

Special Field Order No. 15 reserved, exclusively for black people, roughly four hundred thousand acres of land confiscated from Rebels in coastal South Carolina, Georgia, and Florida. Each head of household was allowed up to forty acres. (There was no promise of mules, but some surplus army mules were distributed at one point.)

Sherman's order stemmed, in part, from a historic meeting on the evening of January 12, 1865, between Sherman, Secretary of War Stanton, and twenty of Savannah's black ministers and church leaders. This meeting took place at Sherman's temporary headquarters: cotton merchant Charles Green's Gothic Revival mansion on Madison Square.

The black attendees included five men who had been born free: James Lynch, age twenty-six; Adolphus Delmotte, age twenty-eight; Alexander Harris, forty-seven; James Porter, thirty-nine; and James Mills, fifty-six.

The group's brilliant spokesman, Garrison Frazier, sixty-seven, was among the men who had been born into slavery. This North Carolina native had purchased his and his wife's freedom in the late 1850s for $1,000 in silver and gold.

After introductions came Stanton's questions.

First: What was their understanding of Lincoln's Emancipation Proclamation?

"So far as I understand," responded Garrison Frazier, "President Lincoln's proclamation to the Rebellious States, it is, that if they would lay down their arms and submit to the laws of the United States

A PICTURE OF HOPE: This illustration speaks to the past and the hoped-for future. On the left are scenes of slavery's horrors (whippings, for example). On the right are scenes of better times for black people in the wake of Emancipation. In the center is a happy, safe family.

before the first of January, 1863, all should be well; but if they did not, then all the slaves in the Rebel States should be free henceforth and forever."

Next question: "State what you understand by Slavery and the freedom that was to be given by the President's proclamation."

"Slavery is, receiving by *irresistible power* the work of another man, and not by his *consent*," Frazier replied. "The freedom, as I understand it, promised by the proclamation, is taking us from under the yoke of bondage, and placing us where we could reap the fruit of our own labor, and take care of ourselves and assist the Government in maintaining our freedom."

Stanton's most important question was this: "State in what manner you think you can take care of yourselves, and how can you best assist the Government in maintaining your freedom."

Frazier didn't miss a beat. *Land!* That's what his people most hungered for. Land and the freedom to be self-sufficient, to live out from under the shadow of their former owners.

What course can be clearer, what course more politic, . . . what course will be so just, so humane, so thoroughly conducive to the

**political weal and the national advancement,
as that the government should immediately
bestow [confiscated] lands upon these freed
men who know best how to cultivate them,
and will joyfully bring their brawny arms,
their willing hearts, and their skilled hands
to the glorious labor of cultivating as their
OWN, the lands which they had bought and
paid for by their sweat and blood?"**

—"What Shall Be Done with the Slaves?" in the November 23,
1861, issue of New York's *Weekly Anglo-African,* established by
black activist Thomas Hamilton

When asked whether black people preferred to live
"scattered among the whites or in colonies by yourselves," Frazier said, "I would prefer to live by ourselves,
for there is a prejudice against us in the South that will
take years to get over."

Four days later, Sherman issued Special Field
Order No. 15.

Secretary Stanton had no problem with the freedmen receiving land; however, he questioned the legality
of Sherman's order. "It seems to me, General, that this
is contrary to law."

"There is no law here except mine, Mr. Secretary,"
replied the general. Sherman was by no means an

abolitionist but a man who very much wanted to be free from the thousands of black people trailing his advance troops. Soon to head off with his army to conquer the Carolinas, Sherman put General Rufus Saxton in charge of land distribution.

"The pews, in the body of the house, were filled," reported the *Savannah Daily Herald* on February 3, 1865, of a meeting in one of Savannah's black churches. There, General Saxton officially gave people the great

GATHERING TOGETHER: A print depicting ill and elderly people lined up outside the Freedmen's Bureau in Richmond, Virginia.

good news about Sherman's game-changing order. "The galleries presented a sable cloud of faces," the *Savannah Daily Herald* went on to say. "Seats were placed in the aisles, and every seat in the house was occupied, and there was still a crowd at the door anxious to obtain an entrance."

After the singing of "America" and prayer, General Saxton addressed the crowd, urging hope and hard work. So did Reverend Mansfield French, a white minister. "They must take their hoes, spades and shovels, and lay out their gardens, and raise vegetables for the market, and chickens, and corn and cotton." That's how the *Savannah Daily Herald* summed up French's remarks.

More aid, more lifelines, were on the way.

In March 1865, the US Congress created the US Bureau of Refugees, Freedmen and Abandoned Lands to aid destitute black and white people in the South. At its helm was "Old Prayerbook": the devout Christian abolitionist General Oliver Otis Howard, a native of Maine. It became known as the Freedmen's Bureau. Frederick Douglass's son Charles was one of the first black clerks General Howard hired for the bureau's office in Washington, DC.

Food. Shelter. Clothing. Hospitals. Schools. Jobs. Parcels of abandoned land. Protection. This was just some of the aid the Freedmen's Bureau provided. Thousands of black people also looked to the bureau to perform legal marriages.

With offices in fifteen Southern states and the District of Columbia, offices staffed largely by soldiers, the Freedmen's Bureau also oversaw the Freedmen's Savings and Trust Company. Congress initially created this bank to help black soldiers and veterans be fiscally responsible. However, in the end, the Freedmen's Bank, as it became known, opened its doors to any African Americans seeking to lay aside dollars and dimes.

Some months ago I complained to your department that Mrs. Charles Strauss and Mrs. Clinch, her sister, to whom I formerly belonged, detained my son Henry, nine years old. Since I had heard that Mr. Chas. Strauss had received a letter from the Freedmen's Bureau ordering the surrender of the child to me but they still detain the child.

—Elizabeth Stone of Newberry, South Carolina, in a March 18, 1867, letter to Robert Kingston Scott, assistant commissioner of South Carolina's Freedmen's Bureau

New Jersey–born abolitionist Tunis Gulic Campbell, Sr., was another black Freedmen's Bureau staffer. Thanks to Secretary of War Stanton, Campbell became "governor" of Ossabaw, St. Catherines, and three other Georgia Sea Islands. "We left with rations and a few families and at Hilton Head got more," wrote Campbell in an April 13, 1865, letter to New York's Freedmen's Relief Association. Among other things, he asked the charity to send books for schools he planned to open.

Campbell's letter was penned four days after General Lee's surrender to General Grant at Appomattox and two days after Abraham Lincoln's last speech.

On the evening of Tuesday, April 11, 1865, on the second-floor balcony of the White House's North Portico, President Lincoln delivered an address on the way forward. "We meet this evening, not in sorrow, but in gladness of heart. The evacuation of Petersburg and Richmond, and the surrender of the principal insurgent army, give hope of a righteous and speedy peace whose joyous expression can not be restrained."

Lincoln warned that the "re-inauguration of the national authority—reconstruction" would be "fraught with great difficulty." But there was hope.

"Some twelve thousand voters in the heretofore slave-state of Louisiana," said the president, "have sworn allegiance to the Union, assumed to be the rightful political power of the State, held elections, organized a State government, adopted a free-state constitution, giving the benefit of public schools equally to black and white." What's more, the Louisiana legislature had the power to grant black men the right to vote. Lincoln hoped that the Bayou State would do that for some.

RECONSTRUCTION CHAMPION: Before he journeyed to the war-torn South, Tunis Campbell supported his family as a waiter at luxury hotels in New York City and Boston. He had also written a book on best practices for working in and running such establishments.

Lincoln said that if he had his druthers, black suffrage would be limited to the "very intelligent" black men and to black soldiers and veterans.

"Outside was a vast sea of faces, illuminated by the lights that burned in the festal array of the White House, and stretching far out into the misty darkness," reported the *Sacramento Daily Union*. "It was a silent, intent, and perhaps surprised, multitude."

"That is the last speech he will ever make," muttered actor John Wilkes Booth, a Confederate sympathizer. Booth was outraged over the possibility of *any* black man having the right to vote in Louisiana or anywhere else.

A few days later, on Good Friday, Booth shot Lincoln in the head as the president sat with his wife and two guests in the presidential box at Ford's Theatre. The play was *Our American Cousin*, an English farce.

Lincoln died the following day at 7:22 a.m. At 10 a.m., his vice president, former slaveholder Andrew Johnson, a Democrat, was sworn in as the nation's seventeenth president.

A native of North Carolina who moved to Tennessee as a young man, the combative, often-crass Andrew Johnson had fiercely opposed Tennessee's secession. A US senator at the time, he was the only Southern senator who did not resign his seat when his state did in fact secede. During the war, once Union forces virtually controlled Tennessee, Lincoln made Johnson military governor of the Volunteer State. Two years later, Johnson became his running mate in his bid for reelection on the National Union ticket.

Two weeks before the election of 1864, on the steps of the state capital in Nashville, Governor Andrew Johnson addressed a pro-Union black rally. Acknowledging that the Emancipation Proclamation

ASSASSINATION OF PRESIDENT A. LINCOLN.

ASSASSINATION: Lithograph showing John Wilkes Booth aiming at the president in his box at Ford's Theatre.

had not declared free the people enslaved in Tennessee (as it wasn't under Confederate control), Johnson proclaimed "freedom, full broad and unconditional, to every man in Tennessee!"

Johnson, born dirt poor, then went on a rant against Tennessee's white elite, a class he thoroughly despised. "Let them gather their treasonable conclaves elsewhere; among their friends in the Confederacy. They shall not hold their conspiracies in Nashville."

After he got that off his chest, Johnson plowed on. "Looking at this vast crowd of colored people and reflecting through what a storm of persecution and obloquy they are compelled to pass, I am almost induced to wish that, as in the days of old, a Moses might arise who should lead them safely to their promised land of freedom and happiness."

"You are our Moses!" people shouted.

Johnson objected, "God, no doubt has prepared somewhere an instrument for the great work He designs to perform in behalf of this outraged people, and in due time your leader will come forth; your Moses will be revealed to you."

"We want no Moses but you!" the crowd cried out.

Johnson relented. "Well, then, humble and unworthy as I am, if no other better shall be found, I will indeed be your Moses, and lead you through the Red

Sea of war and bondage, to a fairer future of liberty and peace."

What would he be to white Southerners who had risen up in rebellion against the Union?

Shortly after Andrew Johnson became president, he told a delegation from Indiana that "treason must be made odious and traitors must be punished and impoverished."

The nation waited anxiously to see what exactly President Andrew Johnson would do.

AFTER LINCOLN: Andrew Johnson, Lincoln's successor, was a tailor by trade.

4

Restored

To say the least, President Andrew Johnson did not turn out to be the Moses who would lead the freed men and women "to their promised land of freedom and happiness." Although he became an opponent of slavery during the war, he would severely disappoint any hope that he would be a committed advocate for equal rights for the former slaves. Indeed, many historians have characterized him as a white supremacist. And when it came to those "traitors"—people who had fought tooth and nail to keep black people in bondage, people who had plunged the nation into a horrific civil war—well, Johnson changed his tune.

Politicians pressed him to keep the Rebel states under military rule for months or years, but Johnson would have none of that. On Monday, May 29, 1865, with Congress not in session, Johnson issued two proclamations that made Radical Republicans erupt in protest.

First came "Proclamation 134—Granting Amnesty to Participants in the Rebellion, with Certain

RESILIENCE: Several generations of a family in Beaufort, South Carolina, who were liberated by Union troops in 1862.

Exceptions." It declared that most of the people who participated in the rebellion would not be charged with treason if they simply swore an oath of allegiance to the United States. Exceptions included high-ranking Confederate officials and Rebels with taxable real estate valued at $20,000 and more. They had to appeal directly to the president for pardons. Though Johnson's sympathies were with poor and middling white folks, he would soon pardon a whole lot of "$20,000 men."

Next came "Proclamation 135—Reorganizing a Constitutional Government in North Carolina." Having tapped Democrat William Holden to be North Carolina's provisional governor, the president instructed him to hold a state constitutional convention with delegates chosen by people loyal to the United States. There were only two things North Carolina had to do to be right with the Union: rescind its ordinance of secession and ratify the Thirteenth Amendment.

This was Johnson's blueprint for reunion across the South.

President Johnson bristled at the word "Reconstruction." On the day he issued his first proclamations, he told John "Black Jack" Logan, "General, there is no such thing as reconstruction. These States have not gone out of the Union, therefore reconstruction is unnecessary." The president added that he did not intend to treat the former Confederate states "as inchoate" or embryonic beings, "but merely as existing under a temporary suspension of their government, provided always they elect loyal men. The doctrine of coercion to preserve a State in the Union has been vindicated by the people. It is the province of the Executive to see that the will of the people is carried out in the rehabilitation of these rebellious States, once more under the authority as well as the protection of the Union."

Well, the war is over, the rebellion is "put down," and we are declared, free! Four-fifths of our enemies are paroled or amnestied, and the other fifth are being pardoned, and the President has, in his efforts at the reconstruction of the civil government of the States, late in rebellion, left us entirely at the mercy of these subjugated but unconverted rebels.

—"Address to the Loyal Citizens of the United States and to Congress," from a convention of black men held in the summer of 1865 in Alexandria, Virginia

Along with Reconstruction, Andrew Johnson also

thought that General Sherman's Special Field Order No. 15 was unnecessary. He gave in to the appeals from white people who used to own the land covered in the decree and revoked Sherman's order in October 1865. Most all of those four hundred thousand acres on the rice coast would be returned to ex-Confederates. The grim task of evicting black people fell to the Freedmen's Bureau.

About forty thousand people had done as General Saxton and Reverend French had urged during that meeting in a Savannah church back in February 1865.

They had taken up hoes and spades and shovels.

They had laid out gardens, raised chickens.

They had readied ground for corn, cotton, and other crops.

They had worked so hard to build new lives and communities on Edisto Island, Tybee Island, Sapelo, Ossabaw, Skidaway, on and on. And now the government was pulling the rug out from under them, their property "restored."

One Freedmen's Bureau document alone listed twenty-eight black families who had their land taken away and "Restored" to a former Rebel. These people lived at Grove Point along Georgia's Little Ogeechee River. There, in the spring of 1865, Dinah Green (family of three), for example, had been given title to fifteen acres; Ned Richardson (family of nine), thirty; and Titus Neal (family of two), ten. Dinah's, Ned's, and Titus's acres and those of their neighbors were restored to Dr. John R. Cheves. During the war his service to the Confederacy included supervising Charleston Harbor defenses and manufacturing incendiary shells.

About a thousand people were living in Tunis Campbell's five-island fiefdom. He had made St. Catherines his base and established a government modeled on that of the United States. Campbell had schools up and running, and a militia too.

Faced with the end of his Georgia Sea Island communities, Campbell did not abandon hope. He purchased the 1,250-acre Belleville plantation on the mainland about fifteen miles southwest of St. Catherines. At Belleville, Campbell established a new black colony.

Few black people facing eviction could do as Campbell did. Many of the Dinahs, Neds, and Tituses wound up working for the restored landowner for a pittance, their hopes and dreams of being self-sufficient, of prospering even, crushed.

It was also in the fall and winter of 1865 that Southern governments began instituting "Black Codes" meant to limit the scope of freedom after slavery while jump-starting the region's agricultural economy by getting the freedmen to return to the fields. In essence, they were instruments of control.

"All persons of color who make contracts for service or labor, shall be known as servants, and those with whom they contract, shall be known as masters," declared a South Carolina law.

To further keep black people economically oppressed, South Carolina allowed black people to be in business for themselves—say, as an artisan or shopkeeper—on one condition. They had to procure licenses from district court judges. These licenses, valid for only one year, forced artisans to pay ten dollars, shopkeepers a hundred. (At the time, a man in Nashville, Tennessee, for example, could buy a pair of boots for about four dollars.)

Black Codes, which began in Mississippi, compelled black people to sign yearly labor contracts with white people, called for them to work from sunup to sundown, and declared those without yearly contracts "vagrants" who could be forced to work. There were pass systems and curfews, too.

To keep black people from being able to defend themselves, other Black Codes banned them from owning many types of weapons. In Mississippi, unless a black person was in the armed forces or had a license from the police board, it was a crime for him or her to "keep or carry fire-arms of any kind, or any ammunition, dirk or bowie knife." People convicted of violating this law would be fined up to ten dollars. Mississippi also made black-white marriages a felony, punishable by life in the penitentiary.

In Florida, black offenders could be whipped. They could also be pilloried, that is, have their heads and hands locked into the holes of a wooden framework erected on a post and left on public display to be ridiculed and even physically attacked.

Black children were not spared. Orphans could be placed into apprenticeships. Poor children who were not orphans could also be placed into apprenticeships whether or not their parents wanted them bound out. Often the new "masters" of these children had once owned them.

Once again, black families were torn asunder.

Once again, black labor was stolen.

When the war closed, our master told all the people, if they would stay and get in the crop, he would give them part of it. . . . Father made us all stay. . . . I never worked harder in my life, for I thought the more we made, the more we

would get. We worked from April till one month to Christmas. We raised a large crop of corn and wheat and tobacco, shucked all the corn and put it in the barn, stripped all the tobacco, and finished one month before Christmas. Then we went to our master for our part he had promised us, but he said he wasn't going to give us any thing, and he stopped giving us any thing to eat, and said we couldn't live any longer on his land.

— Lorenzo Ivy, about sixteen when the war ended, had been enslaved in Virginia

Violence was another tool white people employed to keep blacks "in their place." Black men and women, even children, were beaten up, shot, stabbed, bludgeoned, whipped, strung up for not working fast enough or for failing to be sufficiently deferential to a white person.

"About the 4th of August 1865 one Bill Murray beat the wife and daughters of 'Anthony' (colored) very severely with a stick because they were singing a union song." This is from Freedmen's Bureau agent John Seage's report on white-on-black violence in Rutherford County, Tennessee.

An agent in Texas reported that on November 21, 1865, in Huntsville, a white man named Joseph Rhodes brutally attacked an elderly black man named Caleb. Rhodes kicked the old man "into the fire place, jumped on him and tried to mash him into the fire injuring him most severely. Wanton cruelty and whiskey."

Black people weren't even safe in the capital. In the summer of 1865, a group of whites hurled a black woman from a moving trolley car. They had been egged on by its conductor.

Freedmen's Bureau files bulged with case after case after case of attacks on and murders of black Americans.

As 1865 wound down, there was something to celebrate, however. On December 6, Georgia became the twenty-seventh of the thirty-six states to accept the Thirteenth Amendment. Ratified, it could now be adopted to the Constitution. Slavery was now legally abolished in the United States!

Florida had yet to ratify the amendment abolishing slavery, Mississippi had flat-out rejected it (and would not ratify it until 1995, then not make it official until 2013). And there was Texas. It had not yet held its state constitutional convention. Still, President Andrew Johnson declared the Union restored.

Two days earlier when Congress reconvened, it refused to seat the newly elected representatives and

STALWART RADICAL: Pennsylvania Representative Thaddeus Stevens

senators from the former Confederate states. The Clerk of the House simply left their names off the roll call. This was Congress's first salvo in its war on Presidential Reconstruction.

It was also on Wednesday, December 4, 1865, that congressman Thaddeus Stevens of Pennsylvania proposed forming a committee of six senators and nine representatives to look into conditions in the ex-Confederate states and determine which, if any, merited readmission into the Union.

"The revolutionary schemes of the majority in congress are now fully developed," the *Daily Milwaukee News* told its readers on December 5, 1865. This article, titled "Negro Government or Disunion," is a stark reminder that it wasn't only in the South that some white people suffered from an irrational fear of "black rule" and vehemently opposed justice for all.

"The intention of the radicals," the Wisconsin newspaper went on to say, "is to suppress all serious opposition to their measures by excluding the southern representatives, and then to pass 'an enabling act' prescribing conditions for the 'reconstruction' of the states recently in rebellion."

The Joint Committee on Reconstruction that Thaddeus Stevens had proposed was a go on December 13. Its chair was Senator William Fessenden of

Maine. Among the other senators were Ira Harris (New York) and Reverdy Johnson (Maryland), one of the committee's three Democrats. Thaddeus Stevens, Elihu Washburne (Illinois), and George Boutwell (Massachusetts) were among the committee's House members. These men, also known as the Joint Committee of Fifteen, would hear testimony from 144 people, black and white (including former Confederate general Robert E. Lee), about the political, economic, and social situation—especially concerning black people—in states that had risen up in rebellion.

"Is there no way to arrest the insane course" of Andrew Johnson? That was Thaddeus Stevens in a letter to senator Charles Sumner in the summer of 1865. On December 18, 1865, on the floor of the House, Stevens once again decried President Johnson's policies and justified the action Congress had taken. "Dead men cannot raise themselves. Dead States cannot restore their own existence 'as it was,'" he said. Congress and Congress alone, Stevens insisted, had the power to revive them.

Stevens also argued that Congress was morally obligated to protect freed people. "If we leave them to the legislation of their late masters, we had better have left them in bondage."

Information Wanted!

During and after the Civil War, countless freed people placed ads in black-owned and white-owned newspapers, searching for family—a husband, a wife, children, siblings—lost to them through sale, self-liberation, or in the fog of war.

$200 REWARD—The subscriber will pay the above reward to any one who will bring to him, or to this office, his grandchild, of about five years of age. His father's name was Jacob McKenzie, and his mother's name was Salina. . . . The mother was formerly held by Jacob Barrett of Linton, Ga., and hired to Dr. Carr, of Washington co., Ga. Soon after General Sherman's army entered Savannah, the mother and child started for the same place. At Winsboro the mother was taken sick, and placed the child in charge of a gentleman who had but one leg, and who promised to take the child to Savannah for her. The gentleman's name is unknown; but if the facts stated shall be sufficient to identify the child, the kindness of the one who restores him will ever be remembered in addition to the above reward being paid.

ISAAC WILLIAMS,

50 Wolf St., Charleston, S.C.

—*South Carolina Leader*, December 9, 1865

PETER AND PEGGY VINSON, (COLORED,) of Halifax County, wish to obtain information of their child, named *Emma*, commonly called "*Poss*." She formerly belonged to Mr. Chas. Henderson, of Mississippi, and was bought and left by him in Lincolnton, N.C.

She is dark complected, and about fourteen years of age. Any information will be gladly received by her parents at Brinkleyville,

Halifax County, N.C., or by Caroline Hays, Exchange Hotel, Raleigh
—*Tri-Weekly Standard* (Raleigh, NC), May 31, 1866. Lincolnton, where
the Vinson's daughter was last seen, was more than two hundred
miles away from their home in Brinkleyville.

Information wanted of Mary Buckner, who formerly belonged to
Mary Morrison, in Culpepper County, Va., also of Daniel, Reuben and
George Buckner, formerly belonging to John Miller. Any information
will be very thankfully received by
>   ROBERT BUCKNER,
>   Post Office Box 317, Logansport,
>   Indiana.

—*Christian Recorder*, February 2, 1867. In a subsequent ad, Robert
Buckner said that he had found one relative, Reuben Buckner.

*People placed information-wanted ads into the twentieth century. Mrs. Mollie
Curren of Covington, Virginia, placed one in 1907, more than forty years after the
war ended. Curren was in search of an uncle, Lewis Smith, last known to be in
Arkansas, and her aunts Sallie Anne Thorp, who had married a Spaniard, and Patsy
Thorp. Of her Aunt Patsy, Curren stated: "She was sold during slavery and when
last heard of was living in Louisiana."*

5

The Ballot
with Which to Save
Ourselves

African Americans did more than watch and wait. They organized, brimming with hope for the dawn of a new day.

Alexandria, Virginia . . . Boston, Massachusetts . . . Charleston, South Carolina . . . Detroit, Michigan . . . Harrisburg, Pennsylvania . . . Little Rock, Arkansas . . . New Haven, Connecticut . . . Raleigh, North Carolina . . . Xenia, Ohio—east, west, north, south, all over the nation black citizens held state and regional conventions to discuss the issues of the day and strategize on the way forward. They drafted addresses to the nation for the vote, for citizenship, for an end to the violence, for respect and recognition of their humanity.

"We are engaged in a serious task; we have met here to impress upon the white men of Tennessee, of the United States, and of the world that we are part and parcel of the American Republic." So said Reverend James Lynch at a convention in Nashville in August 1865. "In pursuance of the great work thus begun, we are here . . . to secure for ourselves the full recognition of our rights as men." During the war, this native of Baltimore, who had studied for the ministry at New Hampshire's Kimball Union Academy, engaged in missionary work in Union-occupied South Carolina and Georgia. Lynch was one of the ministers who met with General Sherman shortly before he issued his Special Field Order No. 15.

Especially in the rural South, there were also clandestine gatherings to disseminate information and to bolster peoples' courage to persevere. Many meetings were organized by the pro-Republican Union League during the Civil War. After the war ceased, the league expanded its number of operatives working in the South.

Frederick Douglass, ever the lion, ever taking the nation to task for not living up to its creed, led a band of his brothers to the White House in early February 1866. Surprisingly, President Johnson had granted them an audience.

The men who accompanied Douglass included his son Lewis; entrepreneur George T. Downing, one of Rhode Island's most prominent and wealthiest black residents; and educator John F. Cook, a member of Washington, DC's black aristocracy. The delegation went to the White House to urge the president to get behind black suffrage.

In urging Johnson to support black men having "the ballot with which to save ourselves," Frederick Douglass reminded him that Lincoln had given black men "the sword to assist in saving the nation."

The president countered that if black men secured the vote, there would be violence in the South. "Yes, I have said, and I repeat here," he stated, "that if the colored man in the United States could find no other Moses, or any Moses that would be more able and efficient than myself, I would be his Moses to lead him from bondage to freedom; that I would pass him from a land where he had lived in slavery to a land (if it were in our reach) of freedom. Yes, I would be willing to pass with him through the Red Sea to the Land of Promise, to the land of liberty; but I am not willing, under either circumstance, to adopt a policy which I believe will only result in the sacrifice of his life and the shedding of his blood."

Official: Now children, you don't think white people are any better than you because they have straight hair and white faces?

Children: No, sir.

Official: No, they are no better, but they are different. They possess great power. They

control this vast country. Now, what makes them different from you?

Children: MONEY.

Official: Yes, but how did they get money?

Children: Got it off us. Stole it off we all!

—a catechism in a Louisville, Kentucky, school

While black people were organizing, protesting, petitioning, Congress served up the Civil Rights Act of 1866, a counterpunch to the Black Codes. With the exception of Native Americans living on reservations, people born on American soil were deemed citizens of the nation. What's more, the federal government was duty-bound to protect the property and the lives of *all* its citizens. Congress passed the Civil Rights Act over Johnson's veto on April 9, 1866, a year to the day of Lee's surrender to Grant.

Two months after the Civil Rights Act, on June 13, 1866, something even more momentous cleared Congress: the Fourteenth Amendment. Through it Republicans endeavored to embed citizenship directly into the US Constitution, nine years after the US Supreme Court said in its *Dred Scott* decision that black people never were, and never could be, US citizens.

"All persons born or naturalized in the United States, and subject to the jurisdiction thereof, are citizens of the United States and of the State wherein they reside," said the Fourteenth Amendment. It also declared that states could not deprive citizens of "life, liberty, or property, without due process of law" or deny them "the equal protection of the laws."

Furthermore, the Fourteenth Amendment pressured states to give black men the vote by giving Congress the power to reduce a state's representation if that state denied the vote to any segment of its male population age twenty-one and older.

The amendment also put a check on aspirations of former Confederate leaders. Unless approved by two-thirds of the House and Senate, they could hold no military, civilian, or elected office. (Congress had the option of removing the ban, which it did in 1898.)

Also vexing for the former Confederate states, the Fourteenth Amendment prohibited the federal government or any state from absorbing debts racked up in aid of the rebellion or losses incurred with the liberation of black people.

White violence was a factor in the Fourteenth Amendment clearing Congress. The previous month,

TWO SIDES: A Freedmen's Bureau agent tries to keep the peace.

on May 1, 1866, white people went on a killing spree in Memphis, Tennessee.

Approximately forty-six black adults and children and two white people were killed.

More than seventy people were wounded.

Nearly one hundred black homes were torched.

Twelve black schools were burned.

Several black churches were left in ashes.

WRATH BY FIRE: Dark skies over Memphis, Tennessee, in 1866, as a result of white rage rooted in fear and loathing of Reconstruction and black progress.

"Large sums of [black people's] money were taken by police and others," wrote the Freedmen's Bureau Major T. W. Gilbreth to his boss, General Oliver O. Howard. The thefts ranged from five dollars to five hundred, "the latter being quite frequent owing to the fact that many of the colored men had just been paid off and discharged from the Army."

The thirty-six-hour assault on the black settlements in Memphis came on the heels of an altercation between Irish policemen and black soldiers. A rumor spread that black troops had killed white police officers. In response, the city recorder, John C. Creighton, took to his soapbox on the corner of Causey and Vance Streets. Creighton, reported Gilbreth, "urged the whites to arm [themselves] and kill every Negro and drive the last one from the city." Creighton even prodded white people to "burn up the cradle."

Q: Now state what you know in reference to [your husband] being killed.

A: He came home and said he wanted some supper. I was sick, and said to him that I had nothing in the house to cook him anything from only a little flour .... He went out of the

house to get some meal. In a few minutes after a sister of the church, who lives next to me, came in and said, "Sister Lavinia, Jackson is killed" . . . .

Q: When you went out to see him how did he lie?

A: When I first went out to see him he was laying partly across a log, groaning. I placed my hand on his breast and called him, but he never spoke . . . .

Q: How long did you stay with him?

A: I [stayed] as long as I could, until they told me to go in or I would be killed . . . .

Q: Who told you that?

A: That is what they said on the streets. They said the policemen were going to kill every negro they could catch.

—from Lavinia Goodell's testimony on her husband's murder during the Memphis Massacre

A multitude of black people remained strong in the face of all the violence. Union Army veteran Wyatt Outlaw was among the steadfast souls. In October 1866, he was one of the 115 delegates at the four-day

North Carolina Equal Rights League Convention of Freedmen. Raleigh's African Methodist Episcopal Church was the venue for this gathering of black men representing sixty Tar Heel counties.

Wyatt Outlaw was on the executive board of this equal rights league determined "to secure, by political and moral means, as far as may be, the repeal of all laws and parts of laws, state and national, that make distinctions on account of color."

After the convention, Outlaw formed a chapter of the Union League in his adopted home of Graham. Along with mobilizing folks for political action, this chapter made plans to build a school and a church. Outlaw organized Graham's Union League in his home on North Main Street, which was also the site of his carpentry shop.

Like many other black men and women in their respective communities, Wyatt Outlaw continued to be a positive force in Graham for years to come.

This We Are Going to Use

Before the war ended, a slew of schools for black people sprang up in Union-occupied parts of the South. For example, within days of Sherman's arrival in Savannah, Georgia, in December 1865, Reverend James Lynch received permission to turn two buildings into schools. One had been a Confederate hospital. The other a slave mart.

"It is a large three-story brick building," Lynch wrote of the latter in a letter to the New York Freedmen's Relief Association. "In this place slaves had been bought and sold for many years. We have found many 'gems' such as handcuffs, whips and staples for tying, etc. Bills of sales of slaves by hundreds all giving a faithful description of the hellish business. This we are going to use for school purposes."

After Appomattox, more schools were established all over the South through the Freedmen's Bureau, Northern charitable organizations, and the muscle and money of black communities.

Children and adults alike flocked to these schools, staffed by black and white people, from the North and South.

STITCHING PROGRESS: The Freedmen's Union Industrial School taught women to sew.

6

Go On
with Your
Oppressions

"I am for negro suffrage in every rebel State," said Thaddeus Stevens in the House of Representatives on January 3, 1867. "If it be just, it should not be denied; if it be necessary, it should be adopted; if it be a punishment to traitors, they deserve it."

Stevens's speech was on behalf of a bill with a new plan for reconstructing ex-Confederate states. "Unless the rebel States, before admission, should be made republican in spirit, and placed, under the guardianship of loyal men," Stevens warned, "all our blood and treasure will have been spent in vain."

While debate on that bill continued, Congress remained on the move. On January 8, it gave the vote to *all* male residents of the District of Columbia twenty-one years of age and older. Exceptions included men who had aided the rebellion.

Congress was just getting started.

Over President Johnson's veto, on March 2, 1867, the

bill Thaddeus Stevens championed in January became law. Known as the First Reconstruction Act and as the Military Reconstruction Act, it ushered in "Congressional Reconstruction" in opposition to Johnson's previous measures under "Presidential Reconstruction."

The Joint Committee on Reconstruction had concluded that in their present condition, former Rebel states, except for Tennessee, were not entitled to be in the Union. Under the First Reconstruction Act, ten Confederate states were declared conquered territory. They were put under military rule in five districts.

Commanders of military districts were charged with protecting all people's rights and crushing all violence and disorders. These commanders had oversight over the election of delegates—black men to be among them—to new state constitutional conventions. The new constitutions had to give black men the right to vote and Congress had to approve those new constitutions. What's more, no state would be restored to the Union until it ratified the Fourteenth Amendment (which Tennessee did back in the summer of 1866).

A total of about twenty thousand troops were stationed in these districts:

Military District No. 1: Virginia.

Military District No. 2: North and South Carolina.

Military District No. 3: Alabama, Florida, and Georgia.

Military District No. 4: Arkansas and Mississippi.

Military District No. 5: Louisiana and Texas.

While legions of white Southerners felt trampled upon and only saw miserable, dark days ahead, millions of blacks were full of hope. Finally they would have a voice. Finally they would be able to put forth their vision of the nation's remaking.

Congress further fostered that hope when, on March 23, and again over Johnson's veto, it passed the Second Reconstruction Act. For one, this law put the military commanders of the five districts in charge of elections, starting with voter registration. In July 1867, Congress passed the Third Reconstruction Act. Among other things, it empowered district commanders to remove people from office.

Black participation in state constitutional conventions varied. Take Alabama's, held in Montgomery, November 5–December 6, 1867. Although about 45 percent of its population was black in 1860, of its convention's one hundred delegates, only eighteen were black; however, nearly eighty of its white delegates were Republicans.

Of the 169 delegates to Georgia's convention

GRANT & THE COMMANDERS: General Ulysses S. Grant (center wearing a slouch hat) and General George H. Thomas (to Grant's right) are flanked by the first generals given charge of the ten former Confederate states put under military

rule: Daniel E. Sickles (far left), John Pope (wearing a short beard), John M.
Schofield (wearing a long beard), Philip H. Sheridan (in the forefront with
handlebar mustache), and E. O. C. Ord (behind Sheridan)

(December 9, 1867–March 11, 1868), thirty-seven were black, although black people composed approximately 45 percent of the population in 1860. One student of Reconstruction, retired Marine Corps colonel Samuel Taylor, nevertheless called the delegates "a most remarkable group," adding that it "was more representative of the state as a whole than any other elected body in the history of Georgia, and embodied a

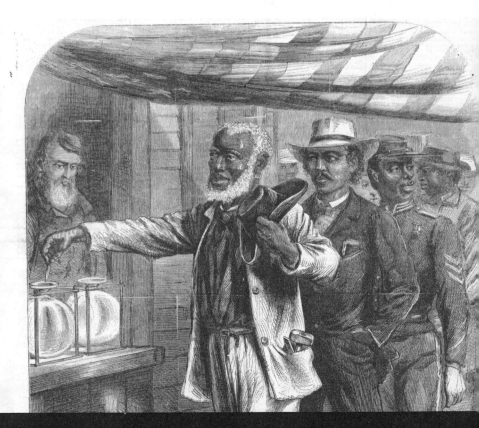

BELIEVING IN THE BALLOT: Black men voting in the October 1867 elections in Virginia. According to the *Encyclopedia of Virginia*, of the state's 105,832 black male residents registered at the time, 93,145 exercised that right.

dramatic shift from antebellum Georgia where the port city of Savannah and the great coastal planters were the economic and political power center."

South Carolina's constitutional convention in Charleston, which commenced on January 14, 1868, and closed on March 17, had the highest percentage of black representatives: more than 70 of its 124 delegates were of African descent. Black people made up about 60 percent of the population in 1860.

"I remarked in a former letter that the colored men in the convention possess by long odds the largest share of mental calibre," wrote *New York Times* correspondent "Q." in late January 1868 of the South Carolina convention. "They are the best debaters; some of them are peculiarly apt in raising and sustaining points of order; there is a homely but strong grasp of common sense in what they say." These delegates included the formerly enslaved Union veterans Prince Rivers and Robert Smalls.

The new state constitution these black men and their white colleagues drafted was quite enlightened and progressive, for both black and white people. It included public assistance for the elderly, the poor, and the disabled, ended debtors' prison, and no longer required an officeholder to be a property owner. South Carolina's new constitution also established mandatory free public schooling *for all* (though, sadly, it would be years before this went into effect). Robert Smalls was among the delegates who really pushed for free public schools. He also advocated women's suffrage.

All in all, of the roughly one thousand delegates to state conventions in ten former Confederate states, more than 25 percent were black men: artisans, farmers, owners of restaurants and grocery stores. Some had been born free, others had been formerly enslaved. They proved just how wrong the president of the Confederacy, Jefferson Davis, and his supporters had been: black people *were* fit to govern themselves. It was a watershed moment in America.

In the summer of 1868, the Fourteenth Amendment became part of the Constitution and seven ex-Confederate states were back in the Union: Alabama, Arkansas, Florida, Georgia, Louisiana, and both Carolinas. Virginia and Mississippi had new constitutions but their citizens had not yet ratified them. Texas's convention was still underway.

Historian Eric Foner estimates that under Congressional Reconstruction some two thousand black men were elected or appointed to public office. They were mayors, marshals, school superintendents, postmasters, city council members, justices of the peace, police officers, sheriffs, state treasurers, state legislators. Sixteen served in the US Congress.

LOUISIANA ALOFT: Oscar J. Dunn, Lieutenant Governor of Louisiana—a first in US history—is surrounded by delegates to the Louisiana Constitutional Convention of 1868.

Those Congressmen included Hiram Revels, born free in North Carolina. On February 25, 1870, this minister and educator who made Mississippi home after the war would become the nation's first black US senator. Also in the 1870s, the freeborn pastor of Mother Emanuel AME Church in Charleston, South Carolina, and newspaper editor Richard H. Cain, would serve two nonconsecutive terms in the US House of Representatives. The heroic

FORGING ON: During Reconstruction and beyond, African Americans continued to hold conventions to draw up plans to secure their rights and improve their lives. This illustration depicts the National Convention of Colored Men's four-day gathering in Washington, DC, in January 1869.

Robert Smalls would also become a national lawmaker. After representing Beaufort in South Carolina's Senate and House of Representatives, Smalls would serve five nonconsecutive terms in the US House of Representatives.

In Graham, North Carolina, Wyatt Outlaw had a say in the running of the local government when he became a town commissioner.

Prince Rivers was a member of the South Carolina House of Representatives, representing Edgefield County, then Aiken County, which he co-founded with two other black men in 1871. Rivers was also a major general in the Palmetto State's National Guard and for a time head of Aiken's Republican Party.

Yet another black man on the rise during Reconstruction was James Lynch, who had been at that meeting in Savannah with General Sherman and Secretary of War Stanton; Lynch started schools there, and made a stirring speech during the black convention in Nashville in August 1865. Lynch made history as the first black person to hold a major political office in Mississippi when he was elected its secretary of state in 1869.

Along with gains there were losses.

On September 3, 1868, the Georgia House of Representatives—dominated by white Republicans—voted to expel twenty-five of its black members. Four retained their seats because, as historian John Hope

Franklin explained, "their fair complexion made it impossible to prove" that they were black.

Go on with your oppressions. Babylon fell. Where is Greece? Where is Nineveh? And where is Rome, the mistress Empire of the world? Why is it that she stands, today, in the broken fragments throughout Europe? Because oppression killed her. Every act that we commit is like a bounding ball. If you curse a man, that curse rebounds upon you; and when you bless a man, the blessing returns to you; and when you oppress a man, the oppression also will rebound.

—Georgia state senator and one of the most dynamic AME ministers, Henry McNeal Turner, on September 3, 1868. Turner, educated at Baltimore's Trinity College, had been born free in South Carolina

A few days after the Georgia House of Representatives' odious act, the Georgia Senate ejected its three black members.

Had these men committed crimes? Had they failed to do their duty?

No.

They were expelled on the grounds that the new

state constitution did not expressly state that black men could hold office.

This was forty-four days after Congress readmitted the Peach State to the Union.

The ousted Georgia lawmakers included Reverend Henry McNeal Turner, who had been appointed as the first black chaplain during the Civil War, Tunis G. Campbell, and Philip Joiner. Shortly after their expulsion, Joiner led hundreds of black people and a few of their white allies on a protest march of more than twenty miles from Albany to Camilla for a political rally. When the marchers reached Camilla's courthouse, whites fired upon them, "killing about a dozen and wounding possibly thirty others," according to the *New Georgia Encyclopedia*.

In March 1869, Congress refused to seat Georgia's senators and representatives. At year's end, Congress put Georgia back under military rule.

Black officeholders who served their communities, their cities, their states, and their nation did so at great peril. Some found it necessary to have bodyguards.

The Ku Klux Klan. The Pale Faces. The Knights of the White Camellias. The White League. The White Brotherhood. The Red Shirts. These are just some of the white supremacist paramilitary organizations that emerged during Reconstruction—men determined to take "their" states back by any means necessary.

On the night of February 26, 1870, a bleak and rainy night—

"Oh Daddy, Oh daddy!" cried Wyatt Outlaw's six-year-old son, Oscar. A gang of sixty or more Klansmen had marched by torchlight to the Outlaw home, then battered down the front door. Once inside, they knocked Wyatt Outlaw's mother to the floor and proceeded to kick and stomp this woman in her seventies.

THE FIRST COLORED SENATOR AND REPRESENTATIVES,

In the 41st and 42nd Congress of the United States.

U.S. Senator H.R.REVELS, of Mississippi   BENJ. S. TURNER, M.C. of Alabama.   JOSIAH T. WALLS, M.C. of Florida.   JOSEPH H. RAINY, M.C. of S.Carolina.   R. BROWN ELLIOT, M.C. of S.Carolina.
ROBERT C. DE LARGE, M.C. of S.Carolina.   JEFFERSON H. LONG, M.C. of Georgia.

NEW YORK, PUBLISHED BY CURRIER & IVES, 125 NASSAU STREET.

PORTRAIT OF PROGRESS, 1872: The first-ever black members of the US Congress gather for a portrait.

With Outlaw in their clutches, they dragged the fifty-year-old widower from his house and beat him as they made their way to an elm tree. They strung Wyatt Outlaw up on a branch that faced the courthouse. A sign affixed to this chest read, "Beware! Ye guilty parties—both white and black."

Wyatt Outlaw's martyrdom was not in vain: after being ratified on February 3, on March 30, 1870, the Fifteenth Amendment became part of the Constitution. "The right of citizens of the United States to vote shall not be denied or abridged by the United States or by any State on account of race, color, or previous condition of servitude," said the amendment with no mention of sex. The amendment also stated that Congress had the "power to enforce this article by appropriate legislation."

Also on that day, Texas gained readmission to the Union. Virginia had gained its readmission in late January, and Mississippi in late February. In July 1870, Georgia would be back in the Union, too.

Now what? With the Union back together, with African Americans bona fide citizens, with black men possessing the vote—"the right by which all others could be secured" as Frederick Douglass once said, would the nation now move forward? Would progressive ideals prevail?

The Great Obstruction

Radical Republicans wanted Andrew Johnson out! They stayed on the lookout for grounds for impeaching the president whom they called the "Great Obstruction." They saw their chance when Johnson fired Secretary of War Edwin Stanton on February 21, 1868, for his allegiance to Radicals in Congress. Within days, the House voted to impeach the president.

The House came up with eleven articles of impeachment. Most stemmed from the Stanton affair. Chiefly, Johnson was charged with violating the March 1867 Tenure of Office Act, which Congress had passed in order to bar the president from firing certain officeholders. Another charge pertained to the president hurling insults at Congress in public.

The trial of Andrew Johnson, the first US president to be impeached, began on March 5, 1868, and lasted until mid-May, when the Senate failed to convict Johnson by one vote. Ohio's Ben Wade was a factor. After Johnson became president, the United States had no vice president, the person who presides over the Senate. Ben Wade had been elected president *pro tempore* (that is, "for a time") of the Senate. If Johnson were thrown out of office, Wade would become president of the United States. And he was too radical for many moderates in Congress.

Legions of white Southerners hooted and hollered over Johnson's acquittal. Some Southern skies were alive with fireworks. Many Republicans in the South made themselves scarce as violent winds whipped up. One Republican in Florida predicted even darker days ahead in a letter to a colleague up North: "News of the failure to convict Johnson will be like Greek fire throughout the entire south. May God save our country from the consuming conflagration."

7

White
Reign of
Terror

"It terrified and subdued Louisiana; it swept over Texas; mounted and disguised ruffians rode through Mississippi in 1871, breaking up the colored schools and driving away preachers and teachers," wrote Eugene Lawrence in "The Ku-Klux Conspiracy," which appeared in an October 1872 issue of *Harper's Weekly*.

Continued Lawrence: "They covered Western Tennessee; they murdered, whipped, and tormented in North Carolina. In Georgia, we are told . . . whole counties of colored voters are disfranchised by the terrors. . . . Not even the Congressional committee has been able to pierce the depths of this widespread conspiracy."

To safeguard black citizens' rights, back in May 1870, a month before the creation of the Justice Department, Congress passed the Enforcement Act. Known as a "force act," it established stiff penalties for voter suppression by anyone, including state officials who tried to keep people from registering to vote based on race, color, or previous condition of servitude. The force act also made it a crime to keep black citizens from holding office and serving on juries.

The president who signed that force act into law wasn't Andrew Johnson, but the hero of Appomattox, Ulysses S. Grant, Republican. Back on November 3, 1868, Grant had defeated the Democratic nominee, Horatio Seymour, 214–80 in the Electoral College to win the presidency. And as historian Brooks D. Simpson has reminded us, this was "the first presidential election where African Americans voted in large numbers in the wake of the establishment of new state governments under the Reconstruction Acts (as well as Tennessee's decision to allow blacks to vote)."

That force act, which Grant signed into law in May 1870, needed backup.

By May 1871, Congress had passed two more force acts. One empowered the president to use military force against terrorists and put lawless places under martial law, which happened to nine South Carolina counties in the fall of 1871. According to Grant biographer Jean Edward Smith, that year, under the watch of Justice Department chief Amos Ackerman, more than three thousand Klansmen were indicted. "Six hundred Klansmen were convicted," writes Smith, "and sixty-five ringleaders imprisoned for up to five years at the United States penitentiary in Albany."

IN CAHOOTS: A figure belonging to the "White League" shakes hands with a KKK member over a shield showing a vulnerable couple and baby. Behind them a man hangs from a tree. Was it possible that conditions were becoming worse than slavery?

When myself and my colleagues shall leave these Halls [of Congress] and turn our footsteps toward our southern homes, we know not that the assassin may await our coming.

—Joseph Rainey in an April 1871 speech in the US House of Representatives urging tougher action against the likes of the KKK

Along with physical violence and threats of violence, black officeholders—and their people—contended with psychological warfare. Black lawmakers were often ridiculed and lampooned in newspapers, presented as buffoons, brutes, and beasts.

Despite the rounding up of white terrorists under the force acts, black voter suppression continued along with violence against black people and white Republicans.

On Easter Sunday, April 13, 1873, Colfax, Louisiana, in the heart of the Red River Valley, became a war zone.

This was in the aftermath of the hotly contested elections of 1872, which resulted in rival governments in Louisiana: a Radical Republican one, and a Fusion ticket of Democrats and conservative Republicans. In early 1873, Louisiana was under Republican rule. And tensions remained high. Those tensions increased after the Bayou State's Radical Republican governor, William Kellogg, removed Grant Parish's sheriff and judge, both Democrats, and replaced them with Radical Republicans.

So on that Easter Day, members of the White League descended upon Colfax, the parish seat. Black men made the town's courthouse their fortress, but to no avail. They were outgunned. The White Leaguers not only fired into the building, they set it on fire. When black men, having laid down their arms, fled the flames under a flag of truce, many were shot dead. Others had their throats cut. A few were hanged. "The total number killed in the fighting and executed afterwards was somewhere between 70 and 165," writes Richard White in *The Republic for Which It Stands: The United States During Reconstruction and the Gilded Age, 1865–1896.* "It was hard to get an accurate account. Men were killed beyond the town; others ended up in anonymous graves."

Three white men died that day in Colfax. In the 1920s, a monument to them was erected in Colfax's whites-only cemetery with the following inscription:

IN LOVING REMEMBRANCE
ERECTED TO THE MEMORY OF
THE HEROES

STEPHEN DECATUR PARISH
JAMES WEST HADNOT
SIDNEY HARRIS
WHO FELL IN THE COLFAX
RIOT FIGHTING FOR
WHITE SUPREMACY
APRIL 13, 1873

It was for the cause of white supremacy that some Southern whites evicted tenants who voted Republican. Businesses were boycotted. Black schools were defunded. People were driven from office. Persecutions were relentless. Some white Republicans, Southern-born and Northern transplants alike, threw in the towel.

"A White Reign of Terror in Louisiana," was the title of a letter to the editor of the *New York Herald*, published in the newspaper's September 3, 1874, issue shortly after white rage erupted in Coushatta, the parish seat of Red River. Here, power-hungry Democrats, members of the White League, killed in cold blood six Republican officeholders—including the sheriff and the justice of the peace—along with several of their black supporters.

"The Vicksburg Riot" was the title of a January 5, 1875, piece in Silver City, Idaho's *Owyhee Daily Avalanche*. On December 7, 1874, when several hundred black men of Warren County, Mississippi, marched on

Vicksburg in protest of the illegal ouster of a black sheriff, Peter Crosby, and other black officials, white men started shooting. "For another ten days, some of the young white participants, joined by reinforcements from across the river in Louisiana, stayed on 'the war path,'" wrote Steven Hahn in *A Nation under Our Feet: Black Political Struggles in the Rural South from Slavery to the Great Migration*. When the violence ended, at least

COLFAX: In the aftermath of the massacre many mourned the losses of loved ones

twenty-nine black people were dead, "and a great many more had been wounded and terrorized."

The reign of terror seemed unceasing.

"Race Feuds in Mississippi," was the title the *New York Evening Post* gave a September 7, 1875, report on a massacre in Clinton, Mississippi. Following a rumor of an impending black attack on Clinton, several hundred members of the paramilitary group the White Liners from nearby towns "just hunted the whole country clean out," a black eyewitness testified the following year, "just every [black] man they could see they were shooting at him just the same as birds." Days earlier, white men had shot up a Republican rally.

The Clinton Massacre, in which some thirty to fifty black people were killed, occurred six months after a landmark civil rights bill cleared Congress.

On March 1, 1875, President Grant signed into law a civil rights bill that outlawed discrimination in places of public accommodation, such as hotels, restaurants, and railroad cars. Offenders could be imprisoned for a year and fined a thousand dollars.

The Radical senator Charles Sumner had introduced this bill five years earlier. "Don't let the bill fail," said Sumner to Frederick Douglass and others gathered around his bed as he lay dying in 1874.

US congressman John Roy Lynch of Mississippi was one of the bill's most eloquent, passionate black backers. A month before the bill passed, Lynch delivered a powerful speech in the House: "I appeal to all the members of the House—republicans and democrats, conservatives and liberals—to join with us in the passage of this bill, which has for its object the protection of human rights." Lynch asserted that when everyone's rights are protected, "then can all truthfully say that this beautiful land of ours, over which the Star Spangled Banner so triumphantly waves, is, in truth and in fact, the 'land of the free and the home of the brave.'"

When the Civil Rights Act of 1875 passed, Charles Sumner was not the only Radical Republican who had died. So had Thaddeus Stevens, for example. What's more, while Republicans formed the majority in the Senate, Democrats, following the 1874 mid-term elections, held the majority in the House.

Ill winds long blowing whipped up into cyclones as the power of Republicans diminished, as white Democrats remained hell-bent on regaining rule in the South, ever ready as always to use violence.

Prince Rivers's majority-black town of Hamburg, in South Carolina's Aiken County, of which Rivers

Eminent Colored Men.

HON. JOHN R. LYNCH,

OF MISSISSIPPI.

COPYRIGHT, 1884, BY J. W. CROMWELL & CO., WASHINGTON, D. C.

TRAILBLAZING REP: Mississippi representative John Roy Lynch later wrote an important personal account, *The Facts of Reconstruction* (1913), as well as other articles that challenged contemporary historians' biased views of the period.

was one of three black founders in 1871, came under attack in the summer of 1876, following a black-white clash on the Fourth of July.

While making their way through Hamburg in a wagon, two young white men, Tommy Butler and Henry Getsen (Getzen in some sources), were inconvenienced by a parade of black soldiers, members of a National Guard regiment, celebrating their nation's hundredth birthday. A vexed Getsen decided to ram the marchers rather than go around them.

The wagon stopped just short of harming anyone.

"Mr. Getsen, I don't know for what reason you treat me in this manner," said Doc Adams, the regiment's captain.

"What?" said Getsen.

"Aiming to drive through my company."

"Well, this is the rut I always travel."

To keep the peace Doc Adams had his men part with the command, "Open order!" That was not good enough.

The next day attorney Matthew Butler (no relation to Tommy Butler) filed a lawsuit, claiming that Adams's men had blocked a public road. Butler wanted the black militia disbanded.

This suit came before trial judge Prince Rivers. After things got heated during the hearing on July 6, Rivers called for a cooling-off period.

When the hearing resumed on July 8, the plaintiffs

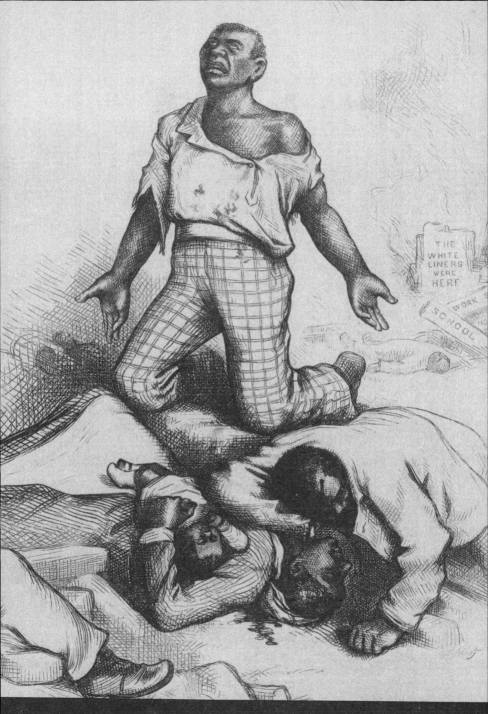

BEGGING THE QUESTION: A man implores the heavens as he contemplates the murdered people below him. The *Harper's Weekly* image invites viewers to consider if the new nation is truly protecting life and liberty.

came to Hamburg with more than their grievance. They were accompanied by armed white men, members of local rifle clubs. Attorney Butler demanded that the militia surrender its weapons. For the cause of peace, Prince Rivers concurred. But the black militia, some eighty to one hundred men, was having none of that and hastened to a warehouse.

Soon, more than two hundred white men surrounded that warehouse. Before long, shots rang out. A battle ensued. White reinforcements joined, including some from nearby Augusta, bearing a cannon. At least one white man and six black men died. There is no record of how many people were wounded during the shooting and subsequent attacks on black homes, including that of Prince Rivers.

"The effects of the massacre spread and galvanized the South Carolina Democratic Party," says historian Richard Zuczek, "while at the same time it drove a wedge between Republicans at the state and federal levels. White Democrats had been divided over the [upcoming] 1876 gubernatorial campaign, with some arguing for an alliance with Republican Governor Daniel Chamberlain as the safest means of achieving victory." As Zuczek goes on to say, "The Hamburg Massacre and its aftermath silenced such talk and catapulted to prominence the 'straight-out' strategy, which supported former Confederate general

Wade Hampton for governor." What's more, Governor Chamberlain's plea for peace-keeping federal troops in the Palmetto State was ignored.

In that same year, Tunis Campbell, who had been such a force for good in McIntosh County, Georgia, and who had been arrested several times on trumped-up charges, was convicted of engaging in corruption while a legislator. The sixty-three-year-old man was sentenced to a year of hard labor.

"On or about the 12th of January, 1876, the guard from the State prison came, about 7 o'clock a.m., and handcuffed me, and with a chain about twelve feet long, dragged me along the streets of Savannah to the Central railroad, and then took me one hundred and forty miles from Savannah, to a prison-camp on the plantation of Colonel Jack Smith's, in Washington county, State of Georgia," Campbell writes in his 1877 memoir, *Sufferings of the Rev. T. G. Campbell and His Family, in Georgia.*

"It is impossible to describe the way in which prisoners were worked," Campbell continued. They were taken out as soon as they could see—both in winter and summer—and kept to work as long as it was light, with one hour for dinner." Prisoners who couldn't keep up with the workload—chopping wood, for example— were "beaten most unmercifully with a leather strop or a buggy trace." These beatings ranged from fifty to one hundred lashes.

The year 1876 also marked one of the most controversial presidential elections in US history. And its outcome would signal the end of Reconstruction.

Economic
Hard Times

In 1873, the world was hit with the first global great depression.
Called a "panic" back then, it would not end in America until the late
1870s.

During the depression, several million people lost jobs, as
factories and other businesses shuttered, as banks went bust. Many
people who held on to jobs only did so by agreeing to wage cuts. The
only work some could find was part-time. As the saying goes, when
white people get a cold, black people get pneumonia.

A major blow to the black community came in late June 1874,
when the Freedmen's Bank collapsed. By then, it had more than
thirty branches in seventeen states and the District of Columbia.
More than sixty thousand customers had trusted the bank with more
than $3 million of their hard-earned money.

White managers stopped making safe investments with
depositors' money and had begun making risky ones (particularly
investments in railroad stocks). Losses on those investments plunged
the bank into deep debt. Not long before the bottom fell out,
Frederick Douglass was invited to be its president. In his effort to save
the bank, Douglass had even invested $10,000 of his personal funds.
Nevertheless, the bank failed.

8

To the Storm, to the Whirlwind

In the year of the nation's centennial, the Democratic Party fielded Samuel Tilden, New York's rather dour, taciturn governor who had waged a valiant anticorruption campaign in the Empire State.

The Republican Party fielded a governor, too: Ohio's Rutherford B. Hayes, a former Union general. The jovial Hayes had generally supported the Radicals when it came to Reconstruction, but as Ari Hoogenboom tells us, by 1876 Hayes had begun "to consider a policy that would allow local self-rule (without military intervention) for the South, if white southerners would respect the political rights of blacks."

The Republican Party only paid lip service to safeguarding the rights of the nation's black citizens in the elections of 1876. The general consensus in the party was that Reconstruction had run its course.

Republicans, not all but enough, were weary—very weary—of Reconstruction. Their weariness stemmed from economic anxiety, charges of corruption throughout a seemingly ever-expanding federal government, the violent killing and wounding of black people in reigns of terror that came with every election season in the South, and a growing feeling that the federal government could not sustain sending in federal troops to quell the unrest. Southern Democrats had been very effective in intimidating black voters with targeted terrorism and sadistic demonstrations of force.

In addition, the Republican Party needed to get its house in order. Back in the presidential election of 1872, there had been a split in the Party. The Liberal Republicans, a faction that favored the end of Radical Reconstruction, nominated *New York Tribune* editor Horace Greeley to run against the incumbent Ulysses S. Grant. Democrats threw their support behind Greeley. Grant won, but the party was fractured. What's more, Grant's administration had been tainted by scandals. In one case, government officials, in league with alcohol distillers and distributors in the Midwest, cheated the federal government out of liquor-related taxes. President Grant's personal secretary, Orville Babcock, was among the men a grand jury indicted as a conspirator in this "Whiskey Ring" in December 1875. A jury later found Babcock not guilty, but the incident bruised Grant's reputation.

The Republican Party not only needed to heal, but also to repair its reputation.

And we should not underestimate the role of the economy. The nation was still in the grips of a depression. Anxiety was running high.

You say you have emancipated us. You have; and I thank you for it. You say you have enfranchised us. You have; and I thank you for it. But what is your emancipation?—what is your enfranchisement? What does it all amount to if the black man, after having been made free by the letter of your law, is unable to exercise that freedom, and, after having been freed from the slaveholder's lash, he is to be subject to the slaveholder's shot-gun? Oh! you freed us! You emancipated us! I thank you for it. But under what circumstances did you emancipate us? Under what circumstances have we obtained our freedom? Sir, ours is the most extraordinary case of any people ever emancipated on the globe. I sometimes wonder that we still exist as a people in this country; that we have not all been swept out of existence, with nothing left to show that we

ever existed. . . . you turned us loose to the sky, to the storm, to the whirlwind, and, worst of all, you turned us loose to the wrath of our infuriated masters.

—Frederick Douglass at the Republican National Convention in Cincinnati, Ohio, June 14–16, 1876

"As the 7th of November, with its great story, approaches," reported the *New York Herald* on November 1, "speculation rapidly increases, and betting on the result becomes more excited. The pool rooms are nightly crowded with an eager throng, including ready backers of the candidates of both parties."

Newspapers made different calls while votes were being counted. On November 8, the *Providence Evening Press* wagered that in all likelihood the next president of the United States would be Samuel Tilden. The following day, Chicago's *Inter Ocean* placed its bet on Rutherford B. Hayes under the headline "Not Yet, Sammy."

There were 369 electoral votes up for grabs. On election night, Hayes had 165. Tilden, who narrowly won the popular vote, had 184 electoral votes. He needed just one more vote to be the victor.

Twenty Electoral College votes were in dispute. One was in Oregon. Nineteen were in three former Confederate states—Florida, Louisiana, and South Carolina, the only Southern states with Republican governments. In these states both parties claimed that their candidate had won. Democrats and Republicans accused each other of ballot-box stuffing and other

COUNTING THE VOTE: On election night November 7, 1876, voters eagerly awaited results.

forms of fraud. Republicans charged Democrats with using bribes and intimidation tactics to suppress the black vote.

The nation was on high alert as it waited for December 6, 1876, the day the Electoral College was to meet.

That day came and went. The election remained up in the air for weeks. During the wait, there were wars of words, physical fights, and fear of another civil war.

To cut through the chaos and confusion, Congress

LATE-NIGHT SESSION: The Electoral Commission conducts a secret meeting on the Louisiana question.

created an Electoral Commission in late January 1877. This fifteen-member decision-making body was comprised of five US senators, five US representatives, and five Supreme Court justices. Seven were Democrats. Eight were Republicans.

On Monday night, February 26, 1877, Republican and Democratic operatives secretly met at Wormley House, a posh black-owned hotel a block away from DC's Lafayette Square. For hours, these men engaged in horse trading, for example, over federal funds for the building of railroads and other infrastructure projects in the South, and over cabinet posts and other high-ranking government jobs. For Democrats the biggest issue was the removal of federal troops from the Louisiana and South Carolina statehouses. These were the last remaining federal troops in the South. They would let Hayes become the nation's nineteenth president if he agreed at long last to remove the troops.

Inauguration Day, March 4, 1877, fell on a Sunday, so the ceremony was held on the fifth. It was a cloudy, slightly snowy day when, on the Capitol's East Portico, Supreme Court Chief Justice Morrison R. Waite administered the oath of office to Rutherford Birchard Hayes.

By the end of April 1877, President Hayes had

DESTRUCTION OF RECONSTRUCTION: This 1877 illustration with its declaration that the Republican Party is dead in the South suggests that the only way a black man might know peace is if he falls in line with the Democratic Party.

ordered federal troops out of the Louisiana and South Carolina statehouses.

White Democrats were beside themselves with joy, ginning up to rule.

On April 22, President Hayes wrote in his diary: "We have got through with the South Carolina and Louisiana [problems]. At any rate, the troops are ordered away, and I now hope for peace, and what is equally important, security and prosperity for the colored people." The president was definitely seeing the South through rose-colored glasses. "The result of my plans to get from those states by their governors, legislatures, press, and people pledges that the Thirteenth, Fourteenth, and Fifteenth Amendments shall be faithfully observed; that the colored people shall have equal rights to labor, education, and the privileges of citizenship. I am confident this is a good work. Time will tell."

In the wake of the Compromise of 1877, Prince Rivers, who had once vowed to die before surrendering the flag, washed his hands of politics and eventually became a coachman again, the role he once had filled under slavery.

Like millions of other African Americans, Rivers, no doubt, braced himself for bleak and midnight days, and the answer to the piercing question Frederick Douglass posed back in 1875 in his speech "The Color Question": "If war among the Whites brought peace and liberty to the Blacks, what will peace among the Whites bring?"

9

Moral
Weakness in
High Places

"The exodus of the colored people from the South still attracts attention," President Hayes wrote in his diary on May 25, 1879. "The effect is altogether favorable."

Fed up with limited employment opportunities, with humiliation and terror—with the overall social, economic, and political oppression—waves of black Southerners packed their bags and headed west.

Most made for Kansas with its abundant, cheap land.

Kansas . . . where John Brown had joined in the fight to keep it slavery-free when it was a territory.

For these people, called Exodusters, Kansas was Canaan, the Promised Land.

One of the movement's leaders was Benjamin "Pap" Singleton of Nashville, Tennessee, a slender man with an iron will, motivated by a grand dream of his people living truly free and independent. Frustrated over the sky-high prices white people wanted to charge black people for good farmland in Tennessee, back in 1873 Singleton made a trip to Kansas. He liked what he saw. He soon led some three hundred residents of Nashville to Cherokee County in southeastern Kansas. There in 1877 he established Singleton's Colony.

"Old Pap," as he liked to be called, a man said to have "full quick eyes and a general expression of honesty, courage, and modesty," passionately promoted moving to "Sunny Kansas." He did this through speeches at emigration rallies where people sang songs such as "The Land That Gives Birth to Freedom," and through a lot of print advertising. In Kansas there was "abundant room for all good citizens," said one flyer, "but no room for loafers."

Hundreds more black people, most from Tennessee and Kentucky, took a chance on Sunny Kansas, and five years after Singleton's Colony was settled there were two more black settlements. One was Dunlap in eastern Kansas's Neosho Valley. By the end of 1878, two hundred families had purchased seventy-five hundred acres of public land and built homes, a school, and two churches. The other colony was Nicodemus, in northwestern Kansas. Nicodemus was not so hearty in 1878, but would soon build up.

CHANGE-MAKER: *(Right)*
Benjamin "Pap" Singleton.

SETTLEMENT STRENGTH: *(Below)*
The rising town of
Nicodemus, circa 1885.

Singleton would later claim that he personally recruited a little under seventy-five hundred black people to Kansas. His reach was far greater, however, thanks to reports of black successes in Kansas and his flyers that blanketed the Southern states. In the spring of 1879, what had once been a trickle became a flood. Thousands and thousands of black people left Louisiana, Mississippi, and other Southern states.

The white people in Louisiana are better armed and equipped now than during the war.

—the formerly enslaved William Murrell to a Senate committee

The Exodus prompted Congress to launch an investigation in which more than 150 black and white people were interviewed. "In the spring of 1879," stated an 1880 Senate report, "thousands of colored people, unable longer to endure the intolerable hardships, injustice, and suffering inflicted upon them by a class of Democrats in the South, had, in utter despair, fled panic-stricken from their homes and sought protection among strangers in a strange land."

The report spoke of people "thronging the wharves

of Saint Louis, crowding the steamers on the Mississippi River, and in pitiable destitution throwing themselves upon the charity of Kansas." Indeed, many of the people joining in the Exodus were not as prepared as Singleton's followers had been. "Thousands more were congregating along the banks of the Mississippi River, hailing the passing steamers, and imploring them for a passage to the land of freedom, where the rights of citizens are respected and honest toil rewarded by honest compensation."

Union Army veteran Henry Adams was among the black people the Senate committee interviewed. Adams, born into slavery in Newton County, Georgia, lived in Louisiana for most of his life. A community organizer, in 1870 he spearheaded the creation of the Colonization Council, a group of black men. The Council—which eventually included about five hundred members—convinced that "it was utterly impossible to live with the whites of Louisiana," petitioned then-president Grant to relocate African American people, possibly to Liberia in West Africa. In 1877, the Council asked the same of President Hayes. When nothing came of these requests, Henry Adams turned his gaze toward Kansas.

When Adams went before that Senate committee,

Ho for Kansas!

Brethren, Friends, & Fellow Citizens:

I feel thankful to inform you that the

REAL ESTATE
AND
Homestead Association,

Will Leave Here the

15th of April, 1878,

In pursuit of Homes in the Southwestern
Lands of America, at Transportation
Rates, cheaper than ever
was known before.

For full information inquire of

Benj. Singleton, better known as old Pap,
NO. 5 NORTH FRONT STREET.

Beware of Speculators and Adventurers, as it is a dangerous thing
to fall in their hands.

Nashville, Tenn., March 18, 1878.

he handed over his notes on black misery in Louisiana, observations made while traveling around the state on fact-finding missions.

While Pap Singleton and Henry Adams urged on the migration, a number of prominent black people opposed it, most notably Frederick Douglass. By then, Douglass was living in Washington, DC, on a fifteen-acre estate, Cedar Hill, across the Anacostia River in Uniontown (later renamed Anacostia). At a time when hope was hard to come by, Douglass argued that black Southerners needed to remain where they were living in the South. In a paper he submitted to a September 1879 convention in Saratoga Springs, New York, Douglass said this: "Not only is the South the best locality for the Negro, on the ground of his political powers and possibilities, but it is best for him as a field of labor. He is there, as he is nowhere else, an absolute necessity."

Another esteemed black person who opposed the migration of Exodusters was a man also born into slavery: Blanche K. Bruce, then a US senator for Mississippi whose wealth included a 640-acre plantation in Floreyville, Mississippi. Bruce bristled at how haphazard the Exodus had become. It sprung, he said, "out of a passion rather than a performance," a passion "pursued impulsively and thoughtlessly, depending upon luck and charity rather than preparation."

Despite the warnings, African Americans continued to go West. Between 1870 and 1880, Kansas's black population alone rose from roughly 16,250 to a little over 43,000. The vast majority of black people, however, remained in the South, where their ancestors had been enslaved.

So many black families toiled as sharecroppers. Under this system, they rented farmland and worked it, agreeing to pay for its use by giving the landowner, in Mississippi, for example, typically 30 to 50 percent of their cotton crop at the end of the year. What's more, under disadvantageous crop-lien arrangements, they had to purchase everything they needed, tools to food, from the landowner's store, pledging to pay for those goods at the end of the year out of the money earned from their share of the crop. In addition to charging inflated prices for goods, the landowner kept the account books. When accounts were settled, most sharecroppers had little or nothing to show for their year of hard work. Many, in fact, began the new year in debt, still owing the landowner money for expenses incurred over the previous year. This was the vicious circle of the sharecropping economy.

Year to year, sharecropping meant children not

attending school because their labor was needed in the fields. It meant contending with a wide range of health risks and even hunger.

Yes, there were some black people in the South who prospered after the end of Reconstruction, including as landowners. As Steven Hahn has noted, by "the turn of the twentieth century, more than one in five African-American 'farm operators' in the South owned some or all of the soil they tilled, and the proportion was considerably higher in certain parts of the region." Things did not, however, get better for most black people in the South.

African Americans all over the nation were dealt a body blow on October 15, 1883, when the US Supreme Court struck down the Civil Rights Act of 1875. In the 8–1 decision, it held that Congress could not stop, say, a hotel or a restaurant from discriminating against someone by refusing them a room or a seat at a lunch counter. The majority of justices deemed the Civil Rights Act of 1875 an overreach under the Fourteenth Amendment, holding that it did not extend to discrimination by private businesses.

The lone dissenter was Justice John Marshall Harlan, a former Kentucky slaveholder who had become a defender of black civil rights. Frederick Douglass was livid.

"We feel it, as we felt the furious attempt, years ago to force the accursed system of slavery upon the soil of Kansas," said Frederick Douglass in a speech at a protest rally in Washington, DC, a week after the Court's decision. It was as grievous, said Douglass, as the 1820 Missouri Compromise, the 1850 Fugitive Slave Act, the 1857 *Dred Scott* decision. The striking down of the Civil Rights Act of 1875 was, charged Douglass, yet "one more shocking development of that moral weakness in high places which has attended the conflict between the spirit of liberty and the spirit of slavery from the beginning."

In the 1880s, black men continued to vote and continued to serve as officeholders, generally in places where black people were in the majority. In 1889, for example, Savannah native John H. Deveaux was made a collector of customs. On the national level, there were still some black men in Congress. Robert Smalls's last term in the House, representing South Carolina, ended in 1887 and three black men—Henry Plummer Cheatham, John Mercer Langston, and Thomas Ezekiel Butler— were elected to the fifty-first Congress in 1889. But things were not getting better. They became worse when Mississippi held a convention to draft a new state constitution in the summer of 1890.

"We came here to exclude the Negro," said the

convention's president, S. S. Calhoon, a colonel in the Confederate Army and a future Mississippi Supreme Court justice.

Calhoon was talking about going around the intent of the Fifteenth Amendment, about suppressing the black vote in a state where black people were nearly 60 percent of the population.

For one, Mississippi's new constitution called for a would-be voter to pay an annual tax in order to vote. This poll tax of $2 was hardly insignificant at the time, especially given that so many people in Mississippi lived in poverty.

Added to the burden of a poll tax, Mississippi's new constitution required that in order for a man to register to vote he had to pass a literacy test: He had to read a passage of the state constitution and explain it. And the registrar could test a black man with a complicated passage while going easy on a white man with a simple line or two. After Mississippi instituted the poll tax and literacy test in 1890, fewer than 9,000 of the 147,000 voting-age African Americans would be registered to vote by 1892.

Other Southern states followed Mississippi's lead, with some lawmakers experimenting with what was known as the "grandfather clause": people could be exempted from the tough new voting requirements if their grandfathers had been able to vote before the Civil War. By 1910, through legislation or through their constitutions, all former Confederate states had effectively disfranchised their black citizens. And in suppressing the black vote with the poll tax, states hurt poor white people, too.

Shameless moral weakness was evident in both high and low places with the rise of the terrorist tactic of lynching black people. These mob murders included hanging people from trees, shooting them in cold blood, and burning them at the stake. Most of the victims were black men and boys, many falsely accused of raping white women.

Others were lynched because they had the audacity to hold their ground. That's what happened in March 1892 to three men connected to the People's Grocery in the Curve, a largely black neighborhood on the outskirts of Memphis, Tennessee. The men were Calvin McDowell (manager), William Stewart (a clerk), and the president of the firm that owned the People's Grocery, Thomas Moss.

W. H. Barrett, a white grocer in the Curve, resented the People's Grocery's success. He went gunning for the store after a black-white brawl in the Curve in which he participated.

The next day, with a police officer in tow, Barrett went to the black grocery store in search of William Stewart, whom he claimed had attacked him the previous evening during that brawl. Barrett ended up knocking Calvin McDowell to the floor with his gun. McDowell got hold of the gun and fired but didn't hit Barrett or the police officer. McDowell wound up in jail until the following day and faced a fine.

"But Barrett took the altercation as an opportunity to create legal trouble for his commercial rivals," Mia Bay wrote in her book *To Tell the Truth Freely: The Life of Ida B. Wells*. Thanks to Barrett, a grand jury indicted the owners of the People's Grocery "for maintaining a public nuisance."

The situation deteriorated after Barrett put out a rumor that white people were going to launch an attack on the black grocery store. The People's Grocery hired armed guards, who in a moment of confusion fired on a group of white men who turned out to be deputies, three of whom were wounded. Along with several other black men, McDowell, Stewart, and Moss—who apparently wasn't even on the scene during the shooting—were arrested.

Then came a rumor of an impending black uprising.

Then came an actual white attack on the People's Grocery.

In the wee hours of the morning of March 9, 1892, a white mob snatched McDowell, Stewart, and Moss from jail. They wound up in "a desolate field just north of the city limits," we read in *To Tell the Truth Freely*. "There they were lined up for execution at gunpoint." After Moss was dead, "at some point the mob gouged out his eyes," wrote Bay, "before leaving all three men stretched out on the ground partially covered with some brush."

Thomas Moss and his wife, Betty, were dear friends of the fearless journalist Ida B. Wells, co-owner of a newspaper in Memphis, *Free Speech*, and a woman who had sued a railroad after a conductor refused to allow her to sit in a first-class car for which she had a ticket. A lower court ruled in Wells's favor, but then the Tennessee Supreme Court overruled the verdict. "O God," she wrote in her diary after that defeat, "is there no redress, no peace, no justice in this land for us?"

After the murders of McDowell, Stewart, and Moss, Wells embarked on a mission to investigate and raise awareness of lynchings. Even though her life was threatened, even though a white mob destroyed her newspaper's offices, causing her to leave Memphis, she refused to be deterred.

In her anti-lynching crusade, Wells produced the pamphlets *Southern Horrors: Lynch Law in All Its Phases*

WRITING WRONGS: Ida B. Wells, born into slavery in Holly Springs, Mississippi, a few months before the Emancipation Proclamation, used the power of her journalist's pen to speak out against injustice.

(1892) and *A Red Record: Tabulated Statistics and Alleged Causes of Lynchings in the United States* (1895), with a preface by Frederick Douglass.

"In slave times the Negro was kept subservient and submissive by the frequency and severity of the scourging," said Wells in *A Red Record*, "but, with freedom, a new system of intimidation came into vogue; the Negro was not only whipped and scourged; he was killed." Wells went on to say, "Not all nor nearly all of the murders done by white men, during the past thirty years in the South, have come to light, but the statistics as gathered and preserved by white men, and which have not been questioned, show that during these years more than ten thousand Negroes have been killed in cold blood, without the formality of judicial trial and legal execution."

How many white people had been tried and convicted for these lynchings?

Wells was only aware of three.

The unstoppable Wells delivered speech after speech on lynchings in the United States as well as in the British Isles.

Between churning out those pamphlets on lynching, Ida B. Wells also collaborated with Frederick Douglass to publish *The Reason Why the Colored American Is Not in the World's Columbian Exposition*

(1893), a stirring rebuke of America's treatment of its black citizens and a praise song to black strides in the face of egregious racism.

The World's Columbian Exposition was the world's fair held in Chicago in 1893, a grand celebration of the four hundredth anniversary of Christopher Columbus's "discovery" of America, one which boasted exhibits from forty-six countries. African Americans who had hoped that their achievements and contributions would be on display were sorely disappointed. The fair's organizers wanted no tribute to, nor recognition of a people that numbered roughly 7.5 million in 1890, nearly 12 percent of America's population.

The Reason Why, with an introduction by Frederick Douglass, included an essay by Wells on lynching, which among other things drove black men from politics. It also included her piece on what she called lynching's twin infamy: the ongoing convict-lease system through which prisons, mostly in the South, rented inmates out to plantations, mining companies, and other concerns. "These companies assume charge of the convicts," wrote Wells, "work them as cheap labor and pay the states a handsome revenue for their labor. Nine-tenths of these convicts are Negroes."

The Reason Why also contained an essay by the

black journalist I. Garland Penn on the progress Black America had made in the mere twenty-eight years since the abolition of slavery, from patents held by black inventors to trained physicians.

With Frederick Douglass, Ida B. Wells distributed *The Reason Why* at the fair's Haitian Pavilion, because Douglass, a former US Minister Resident and Consul-General to Haiti (1889–1891), was representing that nation at the World's Columbian Exposition.

While Ida B. Wells—following in the tradition of Douglass—pressed for full political rights and civil rights, others urged their people to focus on economic development first. Chief among them was a man who became known as the Wizard of Tuskegee: Booker T. Washington, who rose up from slavery to command the great Tuskegee Institute (now University), a vocational and teacher-training school founded in Tuskegee, Alabama, in 1881.

Washington became a sensation in 1895 after a speech he delivered before a mostly white crowd on opening day of another fair: the Cotton States and International Exposition in Atlanta, Georgia. There, on Wednesday, September 18, 1895, seven months after Frederick Douglass died, Washington advanced his philosophy that black people, the majority of whom still lived in the South, would do best to "Cast down your bucket where you are," that is, remain where they were and take advantage of opportunities at hand to acquire skills, money, property, and other tangible assets. "Cast [down your bucket] in agriculture, mechanics, in commerce, in domestic service, and in the professions."

Washington argued that no people "can prosper till it

OUTSPOKEN DELIVERY: Booker T. Washington addresses an audience at Carnegie Hall, 1906. Mark Twain is seated behind Washington in the front row, far left. As a young man, Washington attended Hampton Institute (now University) in his home state of Virginia. He graduated in 1875. Six years later, he was at the helm of Tuskegee Institute.

learns that there is as much dignity in tilling a field as in writing a poem. It is at the bottom of life we must begin, and not at the top." At the same time, Washington advised against protesting the prevailing social and political order. He held that, "in all things that are purely social" black people and white people "can be as separate as the fingers, yet one as the hand in all things essential to mutual progress," that is, economic growth. Washington asserted that "the wisest among my race understand that the agitation of questions of social equality is the extremest folly." Political equality would come in time, he maintained, once black people proved themselves hardworking, independent, upstanding members of their communities. This speech, widely praised throughout the South, would be known as the "Atlanta Compromise."

Booker T. Washington quickly gained the admiration and trust of powerful white philanthropists, including Andrew Carnegie and other industrialists, people who, in turn, made substantial contributions to his school.

Roughly eight months after Booker T. Washington's speech in Atlanta, the US Supreme Court handed down another ruling that devastated African Americans. The case stemmed from Louisiana's 1890 Separate Car Act, which required railroad companies to create "equal but separate accommodations for the white, and colored, races." Those who sat in the wrong car would be fined twenty-five dollars or jailed for up to twenty days.

A group of black citizens in New Orleans, many of them with mixed-race backgrounds, the Comité des Citoyens (Committee of Citizens), decided to challenge the Separate Car Act by having one of its members break the law. That member was Homer Adolph Plessy, a shoemaker who lived in the Tremé section of the city.

On June 7, 1892, thirty-year-old Homer Plessy, who was one-eighth black, boarded an East Louisiana Railroad train bound for Covington. With his first-class ticket, Plessy, who could pass for white, took a seat in the whites-only railway car. When the conductor asked him if he was colored, Mr. Plessy replied in the affirmative. When told to leave the whites-only car, he refused. Plessy was eventually removed from the train and jailed, then quickly bailed out by his fellow committee members.

Everything had gone as planned. The committee had alerted the railroad of Plessy's intent to ride in a whites-only car. It had even hired the detective who arrested Homer Plessy.

His case came before Judge John Ferguson of the District Court of Orleans parish in November 1892, with the judge ruling against him. The Louisiana Supreme Court upheld that ruling weeks later. Plessy's attorneys appealed to the US Supreme Court.

On May 18, 1896, the Court handed down its decision. It upheld Louisiana's Separate Car Act, thereby upholding racial segregation, reinforcing Jim Crow rule.

"Jim Crow" derived from a grotesque character popularized by white entertainer Thomas Dartmouth

DEROGATORY DISPLAY: *(Left)* An 1847 sheet music cover. **COSTUMED ACTOR:** *(Right)* Jim Crow was a character who appeared in stage shows. His persona made fun of

"Daddy" Rice in the 1830s. With blackened face and donning tattered clothing, Rice posed as a bumbling fool of a black man, Jim Crow, in song-and-dance acts.

"We consider the underlying fallacy of the plaintiff's argument to consist in the assumption that the enforced separation of the two races stamps the colored race with a badge of inferiority," wrote Justice Henry Billings Brown in the majority opinion in the *Plessy* decision. "If this be so, it is not by reason of anything found in the act, but solely because the colored race chooses to put that construction upon it."

"Our Constitution is color-blind, and neither knows nor tolerates classes among citizens," said the lone dissenter. Just as when the Supreme Court struck down the Civil Rights Act of 1875, that dissenter was Justice John Marshall Harlan. "In my opinion, the judgment this day rendered will, in time, prove to be quite as pernicious as the decision made by this tribunal in the *Dred Scott* case," said Harlan. He foresaw that the *Plessy* decision "will not only stimulate aggressions, more or less brutal and irritating, upon the admitted rights of colored citizens, but will encourage the belief that it is possible, by means of state enactments, to defeat" the intent, the purposes of the Thirteenth, Fourteenth, and Fifteenth amendments.

Separate schools, parks, libraries, hospitals, hotels, restaurants, restrooms, water fountains, waiting rooms, cemeteries . . .

Separate entrances to theaters, courthouses, and other buildings . . .

Separate seating on trolley cars . . .

The US Supreme Court held that there was nothing unconstitutional about racially separate but "equal" facilities. However, in reality, under Jim Crow, facilities for black people were rarely equal to those for white people.

Whereas a town's white children might attend a finely built brick school, its black children might be consigned to a tar-paper shack.

Whereas white people could travel in well-appointed railroad cars—roomy and with upholstered seats—black passengers on their way to a wedding, a funeral, a vacation, or traveling for work, often had to sit on benches in filthy baggage cars, which often doubled as the smoking cars.

Justice Brown was dead wrong. Jim Crow most definitely tried to stamp a badge of inferiority permanently on black people, despite all the progress they had made since the end of slavery. It clawed, gouged, hammered at their self-esteem, it cut away at their dignity.

At the same time, it reinforced the absurd notion that white people were superior to black people.

Jim Crow had millions of African Americans joining Ida B. Wells's lament: *"O God, is there no redress, no peace, no justice in this land for us?"*

10
Mighty Current

D espite Jim Crow's long reign, against daunting, mountainous odds, African Americans persevered. They pressed on with their ambitions to attend college, get an education, own a home, or start a business. A multitude of proud, determined men and women also gave of their time and of their treasure to groups devoted to racial uplift and to pushing back against the negative stereotypes of black people so pervasive during the Jim Crow era.

So many refused to be defeated.

So many refused to give up on the hope that their country one day would live up to the glorious idea that all people are created equal, that all people deserve to live unfettered and free.

So many essentially had as their motto that of a school Nannie Burroughs would open in Washington, DC, in 1909: "We Specialize in the Wholly Impossible."

It was in Washington, DC, in July 1896—two months after the *Plessy* decision—that black women formed the National Association of Colored Women (NACW). NACW was a merger of the National Federation of Afro-American Women, founded in Boston, and the National League of Colored Women, headquartered in DC.

Josephine St. Pierre Ruffin spearheaded the conference. Founding the Woman's Era Club and the *Woman's Era*, the nation's first newspaper aimed at black women, are just two of her achievements.

Joining Ruffin in the formation of the NACW were Ida B. Wells, writer Frances E. W. Harper, Harriet Tubman (then in her seventies), and Victoria Earle Matthews, soon to found the White Rose Mission, a settlement house in New York City.

NACW's first president was Mary Church Terrell, daughter of the prominent Memphis businessman Robert Church. Terrell, fluent in French, German, and Italian, had earned her bachelor's and master's degrees from Oberlin College, then lived in Europe for two years. She had recently been appointed to the Washington, DC, Board of Education when elected the NACW's first president.

As an umbrella organization for black women's clubs around the nation, NACW raised money for schools, libraries, and charities, as well as for concerts and other cultural events. NACW raised awareness of racial wrongs, from lynchings to black voter suppression in the South. It also campaigned for women to have the national vote (not achieved until 1920). The organization, still a powerhouse today as the National Association of Colored Women's Clubs (NACWC), took as its motto "Lifting as We Climb."

Black men were hardly idle. In March 1897, a small group of intellectuals established the American Negro Academy (ANA), a literary society and think tank. Founding members included the Northern-born

MARY CHURCH TERRELL: Another regal dynamo.

debonair W. E. B. Du Bois, a graduate of Fisk University in Nashville, Tennessee, and the first black person to earn a PhD from Harvard University (1895). At the time of the ANA's founding, Du Bois was a professor at Atlanta University (now Clark Atlanta), like Fisk, another historically black school created during Reconstruction. The publication of Du Bois's seminal collection of essays, *The Souls of Black Folk*, was six years away.

The princely Episcopal priest Alexander Crummell

was the ANA's president. Born free in New York City in 1819, Crummell earned his bachelor's degree in England, at the University of Cambridge in 1853. He went on to teach at Liberia College in Liberia, West Africa, where he lived for twenty years.

The papers that the ANA produced include "The Status of the Free Negro Prior to 1860" by Lafayette M. Hershaw, a Washington, DC, civil servant and journalist. Another is "The Economic Contribution by the Negro in America" by New York bibliophile Arthur Schomburg. This Afro–Puerto Rican man's collection of black-history related books, pamphlets, and ephemera became the foundation for today's Schomburg Center for Research in Black Culture, a branch of the New York Public Library located in Harlem, New York.

ANA members, like other black strivers, did not merely want their nation to recognize what their people were capable of. They wanted the whole world to know. For this cause, in the spring of 1900, Du Bois headed to the world's fair in Paris, France.

When Congress funded the exposition's American Pavilion, there was no thought of including anything about black contributions and achievements. Du Bois's fellow Fisk alum Thomas Calloway, an attorney working at the War Department, raised a ruckus. He

UNITED TOGETHER: Officers of the Women's League, strong and ready, in Newport, Rhode Island, circa 1899.

received tremendous support from US representative George Henry White of North Carolina, the last black member of Congress to serve at the dawn of the new century and a man on fire for anti-lynching legislation and an end to the disenfranchisement of black men. White fought hard for Black America to be represented at that world's fair in Paris. Owing to his efforts, Congress allocated $15,000 for an exhibit on African Americans. Calloway turned to Du Bois for a display on the achievements of black people in Georgia. Calloway chose the Peach State because it had "the largest negro population and because it is a leader in Southern sentiment."

To the Paris Exposition ... thousands upon thousands will go, and a well selected and prepared exhibit, representing the Negro's development in his churches, his schools, his homes, his farms, his stores, his professions and pursuits in general will attract attention ... and do a great and lasting good in convincing thinking people of the possibilities of the Negro.

—Thomas Calloway in an October 1899 letter to more than a hundred prominent black citizens

Du Bois won a gold medal for his exhibit, pulled together in a matter of a few months, a display he called "an honest, straightforward exhibit of a small nation of people, picturing their life and development without apology or gloss, and above all made by themselves." His wondrous work included hundreds of photographs bearing witness to black successes against the odds, not all of them taken in Georgia. There was, for example, a photograph of the board of directors of a manufacturing company in Concord, North Carolina, and of S. J. Gilpin's shoe store in Richmond, Virginia.

Images of proud, resourceful, accomplished, and dignified black people nicely dressed and well-groomed, were a powerful counter to the proliferating "Sambo" art: images on ads, books, postcards, and knickknacks depicting black people with exaggerated features, often up to no good: men stealing chickens, for example, or lustily devouring watermelons. Some items bore images of grinning black children about to be devoured by alligators and of black women looking rather daft and pleased as punch to serve white people. The photographs Du Bois displayed in Paris said, *No! That is not who we are!*

COLLEGE WOMEN: *(Top)* Students seated on the steps of a building on Atlanta University's campus, circa 1900.

HIGHER EDUCATION: *(Bottom)* Graduating law students at Howard University celebrate their achievement, circa 1900.

Lift every voice and sing

Till earth and Heaven ring,

Ring with the harmonies of liberty;

Let our rejoicing rise

High as the listening skies,

Let it resound loud as the rolling sea.

Sing a song full of the faith that the dark
past has taught us,

Sing a song full of the hope that the
present has brought us,

Facing the rising sun of our new day begun

Let us march on till victory is won.

—the first stanza of "Lift Every Voice and Sing," the National
Black Anthem. Written by James Weldon Johnson and set to music
by his brother J. Rosamond Johnson, this song was first per-
formed by five hundred children in Jacksonville, Florida, on
February 12, 1900, as part of a celebration of Abraham Lincoln's
birthday.

By the time Du Bois returned from the Paris Exposition Universelle, that lone black US congressman, George Henry White, first elected to Congress in 1897, had decided not to seek another term. "The onslaught of white supremacy in his home state assured White that to campaign for a third term would be fruitless," explains a brief biography of the man on a US House of Representatives' website.

On January 29, 1901, White bid his colleagues in the Capitol adieu. And not with a whimper, but with sound and fury.

"This, Mr. Chairman, is perhaps the negroes' temporary farewell to the American Congress," said White, "but let me say, Phoenix-like he will rise up someday and come again. These parting words are in behalf of an outraged, heart-broken, bruised, and bleeding, but God-fearing people, faithful, industrious, loyal people—rising people, full of potential force."

In leaving Congress, White did not leave the field in terms of helping them rise. He served his people as a lawyer in Washington, DC, and later in Philadelphia. White also helped establish a black town in New Jersey, Whitesboro, to prove that, "self-sufficient blacks could not only survive but flourish, if . . . left alone in a neutral, healthy environment."

W. E. B. Du Bois became even more engaged in the campaign for racial justice for that "small nation of people."

In February 1905, Du Bois and William Monroe Trotter invited about sixty black men to a conference. It was held July 11–13 at the Erie Beach Hotel on the Canadian side of Niagara Falls.

The twenty-nine men who answered the call hailed from fourteen states. They included Alonzo F. Herndon, who had been born into slavery. This man who began life with nothing owned several barbershops in Atlanta, one of which featured chandeliers and gold fixtures. Herndon had recently launched what became the Atlanta Life Insurance Company and was on his way to becoming the city's wealthiest black resident. His son Norris B. Herndon would become one of Harvard Business School's first black graduates.

Also there was the conference co-organizer, the hot-tempered William Monroe Trotter of Boston. The son of James Monroe Trotter, a Union Army veteran and a man of means, he was the first black Harvard man elected to Phi Beta Kappa, graduating magna cum laude in 1895. In 1901, Trotter had founded a newspaper he named the *Guardian*. Its motto: "For Every Right, With All Thy Might!"

Du Bois, Herndon, Trotter, and the other men of mark

who met at the Falls formed the Niagara Movement, so named for the place of its founding and for the "mighty current" of change they endeavored to bring about in their protest of Jim Crow and other injustices. The Niagara Movement was also pledged to unleash a mighty current of protest against the Wizard of Tuskegee's philosophy.

By then, Booker T. Washington had a vast network of operatives promoting his philosophy, known as "the Tuskegee Machine." With the ear of white

FOUNDING MEMBERS: Originators of the Niagara Movement are superimposed over an image of Niagara Falls. Herndon is top row, second from left. Du Bois is in the second row, third from the left.

philanthropists and politicians, Washington could secure jobs for loyalists and steer funds to schools and other organizations in step with his thinking. He could also hurt the prospects of people and organizations not in line with him. That said, in reality a host of black men and women were very much in line with Washington, genuinely believing that economic development ought to be their peoples' primary focus. Surprisingly, Washington also secretly supported some progressive political causes.

By 1907, the Niagara Movement had thirty branches with three hundred members. There was also a Junior Niagara Movement for college men and recent college graduates.

Resolved, that the Negro Race in America now needs fearless, upright, uncompromising leaders.

Resolved, that is it detrimental to the interest of any race to give up on political rights for the sake of immediate pecuniary gain.

—two suggested topics of discussion in a Junior Niagara Movement recruiting pamphlet

By 1910, the Niagara Movement splintered when several of its members joined a new group: the interracial National Association for the Advancement of Colored People (NAACP), which would become the nation's largest civil rights organization.

The NAACP was born of yet another white-on-black rampage, this one in the North, in Springfield, Illinois, Abraham Lincoln's adopted hometown. There on the steamy early evening of August 14, 1908, white men gathered at the county jail intent on lynching George Richardson, a black construction worker locked up that day after a white woman falsely accused him of sexual assault. There was another black man in that jail: Joe James, arrested in July for the murder of a white man. With trouble brewing, Sheriff Charles Werner had both black men transferred to a jail some sixty miles away from Springfield. When angry white men learned of this, they went wild.

"The eastern sky is lurid with the reflection of raging fires," reported the *Illinois State Journal* on August 15 of the destruction of a mostly black neighborhood.

"'Lincoln freed you, we'll show you where you belong,' was one of the cries with which the Springfield mob set about to drive the negroes from town." So began the article "The Race War in the North" by white journalist and reformer William English

Walling. With his wife, Anna Strunsky, Walling had rushed to Springfield as soon as news of the violence reached them in Chicago.

"The mob was composed of several thousand of Springfield's white citizens," wrote Walling, "while other thousands, including many women and children, and even prosperous business men in automobiles, calmly looked on, and the rioters proceeded hour after hour and on two days in succession to make deadly assaults on every negro they could lay their hands on, to sack and plunder their houses and stores, and to burn and murder."

By the night of August 16, Illinois National Guardsmen had Springfield under control. When the smoke cleared, four white men were dead and two black men had been lynched. Scores of people were injured.

"Yet who realizes the seriousness of the situation, and what large and powerful body of citizens is ready to come to [black peoples'] aid?" Walling agonized at the end of "The Race War in the North," which ran in a New York City newspaper, the *Independent*, on September 3, 1908.

Five months later, on February 12, 1909, the centennial of Lincoln's birth, sixty *extremely* concerned citizens released a "call" for a conference on the fight for racial justice that spring in New York City. Thus, the origins of the NAACP.

The majority of the men and women who signed that call were white. Along with William English Walling, they included millionaire John E. Milholland; Mary White Ovington, co-founder of the Greenpoint Settlement in Brooklyn, New York; and Lillian Wald, founder of the Henry Street Settlement House in lower Manhattan. There was also a grandson of the fiery abolitionist William Lloyd Garrison, Oswald Garrison Villard, editor of the *New York Evening Post*. Ida B. Wells was one of the seven black people who signed. W. E. B. Du Bois was another.

In 1910, Du Bois launched the NAACP's monthly magazine, *The Crisis*. Its mission was to "set forth those facts and arguments which show the danger of race prejudice, particularly as manifested to-day toward colored people." In fulfilling its mission, *The Crisis* offered readers national and international news. It alerted them to must-read books. It shone the spotlight on black achievements and possibilities.

The *Chicago Defender* was another organ of pride and protest. Attorney Robert Sengstacke Abbott, a native of St. Simons Island, Georgia, whose parents had been enslaved, launched this weekly newspaper in 1905. Other leading black newspapers of the day included the Harlem-based *Amsterdam News* and the *Pittsburgh Courier*.

The black press was a lifeline, a rescue for a despised people in a nation still flooded with items bearing insulting images of black men and women, girls and boys. Dolls, fans, postcards, figurines, advertisements, utensils, coin banks, sheet music, planters, toys—all were used to promote stereotypes of black people,

MOVIE MADNESS: In a scene from D. W. Griffith's controversial 1915 film, *The Birth of a Nation*, members of the Ku Klux Klan charge on black soldiers. The NAACP denounced the film for its racist portrayal of African Americans. In Boston, William Monroe Trotter, who in 1908 had launched the National Equal Rights League, led a mass protest march.

propagating the lie that black people were not beautiful or intelligent.

D. W. Griffith's blockbuster *The Birth of a Nation* was a monumental outrage. Originally released in early February 1915 under the title *The Clansman* (the title of Thomas Dixon's novel on which the film was based), *The Birth of a Nation* presented a distorted, racist view of Reconstruction, as a wildly chaotic, unruly, and corrupt time. The film demonized black people and white Republicans. It glorified the Ku Klux Klan. President Woodrow Wilson, a Democrat, was one of the film's fans. In a letter to D. W. Griffith, Wilson called *The Birth of a Nation* "a splendid production." A native of Virginia, Wilson was the first Southerner to occupy the White House since Andrew Johnson.

When he ran for president, Woodrow Wilson courted the black vote, earning the support of Du Bois and other black leaders. Once in office, Wilson proved to be a false friend. A month after he was sworn in as the nation's twenty-eighth president, Wilson signed off on the re-segregation of federal government agencies.

From the Post Office to the Treasury Department, black workers contended with separate but unequal restrooms, cafeterias, work spaces. With the advent of Jim Crow in government agencies, black federal employees also faced a wave of firings and demotions.

"Sir, you have now been President of the United States for six months and what is the result?" raged Du Bois in a September 1913 open letter to Woodrow Wilson, a letter that ran in *The Crisis*. "It is no exaggeration to say that every enemy of the Negro race is greatly encouraged; that every man who dreams of making the Negro race a group of menials and pariahs is alert and hopeful."

Seven months after *The Birth of a Nation*'s release, the resolute Carter G. Woodson, the second black person to earn a PhD from Harvard (in history, 1912), laid the groundwork for an organization to research and trumpet black history and culture: the Association for the Study of Negro Life and History, today's Association for the Study of African American Life and History (ASALH).

"We have a wonderful history behind us," Woodson would one day proclaim in a speech at Hampton Institute. He followed his proclamation with a caution: "If you are unable to demonstrate to the world that you have this record, the world will say to you, 'You are not worthy to enjoy the blessings of democracy or anything else.' They will say to you, 'Who are you anyway?'"

After founding the Association and operating out of a three-story Victorian row house in Northwest DC,

Woodson went on to produce a raft of groundbreaking books, most notably the nearly four-hundred-page textbook *The Negro in Our History* (1922) and *The Mis-Education of the Negro* (1933). Woodson also published the periodicals *Journal of Negro History* and *Negro History Bulletin*. In February 1926, Woodson launched

THE FATHER OF BLACK HISTORY: Carter Godwin Woodson (circa 1905) born in New Canton, Virginia, to parents who had been born into slavery.

Negro History Week, precursor of Black History Month. He is known as the father of black history.

Woodson's Association was born in early September 1915, when the scholar was visiting Chicago. There, at a black YMCA on Wabash Avenue, he called a meeting of like-minded men to hammer out the formation of an organization that would refute the widespread myth that African Americans came from a "nothing people," and were a "nothing people."

Like thousands of other black people, Woodson and his mates were in Chicago for the Lincoln Jubilee: the August 22–September 16 celebration of the fiftieth anniversary of the abolition of slavery in the United States. The Jubilee was held at the Coliseum in the city soon to be a mecca for a multitude of black people leaving the South in search of better jobs, better schools, better lives in the urban North as part of the Great Migration. That migration—beginning in the 1890s—picked up steam during World War I and continued well into the century.

During the Jubilee's opening ceremonies a band played "My Country 'Tis of Thee."

"The exposition takes the negro at 1860 when there were 4,441,730 of his color in the United States, 90 percent illiterate," reported the *Chicago Tribune* on August 22, 1915, "and traces his progress in education, religion, agriculture, industry, art, literature, commerce, sociology, and miscellaneous pursuits up to the year 1915, when the negro population is 9,828,000 and has 400 schools and 31,000 churches, with illiteracy reduced to 30.5 per cent."

Black patriots of the American Revolution . . . the inventions of Elijah McCoy . . . nailless furniture by Adelbert Lee . . . faculty members of the oldest private historically black university founded by African Americans, Wilberforce, in Xenia, Ohio . . . members of the Dewmaine, Illinois, Mine Rescue Corps . . . the business brains of Annie Turnbo Malone, a chemist with a beauty care company, Poro, headquartered in St. Louis, Missouri, a woman on her way to becoming a millionaire . . .

This was a sampling of black pride on display at the Lincoln Jubilee.

On view, too, was the work of Henry O. Tanner, best known for the paintings *The Banjo Lesson* and *The Thankful Poor*. The sculpture *Awakening of Ethiopia* by the lesser-known Fannie M. Stout was also there.

In his booth, Carter G. Woodson sold photographs of Sojourner Truth, Frederick Douglass, and other history makers. It was the sights and sounds—the whole wondrousness of the Jubilee—that inspired Woodson to launch his Association.

"The crowning social event," reported Chicago's *Broad Ax*, a black-owned weekly, came on Thursday evening August 26: a ball "attended by more than two thousand people and when it wound up more than fifty automobiles stood ready, to convey many of the elegantly costumed ladies and the merry dancers to their homes."

Of course these merry revelers awoke on the morrow beneath Jim Crow clouds, for the invidious system was not limited to the South. And Jim Crow ruled and reigned by law and custom in America for many more years, deep into the twentieth century.

FACES OF THE FUTURE 1899: Preschoolers in Tennessee Town, a black neighborhood in Topeka, Kansas.

At the beginning of the century some white scholars cast Reconstruction as a terrible time in American history, a time when ruthless, vicious white Republicans in league with vile, ignorant black Republicans tried to subjugate "noble" white Southerners. These historians were members of the Dunning School, named after the man who mentored them: William Archibald Dunning, a professor at Columbia University, who published his book on Reconstruction in 1907.

But Reconstruction had its champions. It was also in the twentieth century that other scholars pushed back against myths about Reconstruction. One was W. E. B. Du Bois with his 1935 tome *Black Reconstruction: An Essay Toward a History of the Part Which Black Folk Played in the Attempt to Reconstruct Democracy in America, 1860–1880.*

"The slave went free; stood a brief moment in the sun; then moved back again toward slavery."

So wrote Du Bois of Reconstruction's destruction, which gave rise to the Jim Crow era that in turn sent the nation on a backward course from its ideals, its possibilities, its promise. But all was not lost.

Just as it was in the past, so it would be in the 1920s, 1930s, 1940s, and beyond, as a host of black people in America flat-out refused to be defeated, to accept the status quo. So many embraced the idea in a Langston Hughes 1920s poem: "I, Too, Sing America."

With a legion of allies across the color line, they continued to strive for a just America. In keeping with the National Black Anthem, "Lift Every Voice and Sing," they told their children that the dark days would not last.

They entreated their children to believe in the listening skies.

They rallied them to get ready to face the rising sun.

To march on till victory was won, a victory that included the triumphs of Reconstruction, most especially the Thirteenth, Fourteenth, and Fifteenth Amendments to the US Constitution.

Acknowledgments

We would like to thank the countless dedicated and intelligent people who contributed their time, expertise, and passion to this book.

We are grateful to the Core Book Research Team at the Hutchins Center for African & African American Research at Harvard—Dr. Kevin M. Burke, Director of Research; Dr. Sheldon Cheek, Assistant Director of the Image of the Black Archive & Library; and Dr. Robert Heinrich, Non-Resident Fellow of the W. E. B. Du Bois Research Institute—for their invaluable scholarly reads and contributions to the manuscript. Thank you for your beautiful minds and depth of knowledge!

Thank you to Dr. Abby Wolf, Executive Director, and Amy Godsdanian, Executive Assistant, of the Hutchins Center, who have both been incredible ongoing sources of strength and support.

For their expertise in curating the images that help the text come to life, we owe great thanks to Dr. Rhae Lynn Barnes, Assistant Professor of History at Princeton University; Dr. David Bindman, Fellow at the Hutchins Center and Professor Emeritus of Art History, University College

London; and Dr. Adrienne L. Childs, independent scholar, art historian, and curator, and Associate of the W. E. B. Du Bois Research Institute at the Hutchins Center.

We are grateful for the love and support of family and friends, Dr. Marial Iglesias Utset; Liza, Maggie, Aaron, and Ellie Gates; Sarah Colamarino; Glenn Hutchins; Earl Lewis; Dyllan McGee; Michael Sneed; and Darren Walker.

We thank the production team for the PBS documentary film series about Reconstruction: Dyllan McGee, Deborah Porfido, Robert Yacyshyn, Mark Weigel, Jennifer Weigel, Julia Marchesi, Asako Gladsjo, Rob Rapley, Cyndee Readdean, Stacey Holman, Kevin Burke, Veronica Leib, Christine Allen, Judson Wells, Ines Farag, Alexis Williams, Willy Fines, Yah-Mari Cole, Judy Aley, Hampton Carey, Kelsi Lindus, Kate Gill, and David Raphael. This project could not have gotten off the ground without funders Johnson & Johnson, the Corporation for Public Broadcasting, the Gilder Foundation, Dr. Georgette Bennett and Dr. Leonard Polonsky, CBE, the Andrew W. Mellon Foundation, and the Ford Foundation. We'd also like to thank the many scholars who informed the series on and off camera, including our key series advisor, Eric Foner, and core advisors, Rhae Lynn Barnes, Gregory Downs, Steven Hahn, and Kate Masur.

We are grateful to our agents, David Kuhn, Lauren Sharp, and Jennifer Lyons, whose love and care brought this book to our editor Andrea Davis Pinkney at Scholastic, whose enthusiasm is downright infectious (and whose organizational skills are awesome).

In addition, we'd like to thank the hardworking team at Scholastic who made the book a reality: associate editor Natalia Remis for helping to keep things on track; photo researcher Amla Sanghvi for all the terrific finds; copyeditor Bonnie Cutler for her eagle eyes; and Len Small for that wondrous designing mind. And to art director Keirsten Geise and production team Jael Fogle and Erin O'Connor, thank you for being in the trenches with this book from day one.

—HLG & TB

Selected Sources

Alexander, Shawn Leigh. *An Army of Lions: The Civil Rights Struggle Before the NAACP*. Politics and Culture in Modern America. Philadelphia: University of Pennsylvania Press, 2012.

———. *W. E. B. Du Bois: An American Intellectual and Activist*. Library of African-American Biography. Lanham, MD: Rowman & Littlefield, 2015.

Ancestry.com. *The Freedmen's Bureau Online: Records of the Bureau of Refugees, Freedmen and Abandoned Lands*, http://www.freedmensbureau.com.

Ash, Stephen V. *A Massacre in Memphis: The Race Riot That Shook the Nation One Year after the Civil War*. New York: Hill and Wang, 2013.

———. *Firebrand of Liberty: The Story of Two Black Regiments That Changed the Course of the Civil War*. New York: W. W. Norton & Co., 2008.

Ayers, Edward L. *The Promise of the New South: Life after Reconstruction*. New York: Oxford University Press, 2007. 15th anniversary ed.

———. *The Thin Light of Freedom: The Civil War and Emancipation in the Heart of America*. New York: W. W. Norton & Co., 2017.

Ballard, John H. *Lincoln Jubilee Album: 50th Anniversary of Our Emancipation, Held in Chicago August 22d to September 16th, 1915*. Chicago: n.p., 1915.

Bay, Mia. *To Tell the Truth Freely: The Life of Ida B. Wells*. New York: Hill & Wang, 2010.

Berlin, Ira, Joseph P. Reidy, and Leslie S. Rowland, eds. *Freedom's Soldiers: The Black Military Experience in the Civil War*. New York: Cambridge University Press, 1998.

Blassingame, John W., ed. *Slave Testimony: Two Centuries of Letters, Speeches, Interviews, and Autobiographies*. Baton Rouge: Louisiana State University Press, 1977.

Blight, David W. *Frederick Douglass: Prophet of Freedom*. New York: Simon & Schuster, 2018.

————. *Frederick Douglass' Civil War: Keeping Faith in Jubilee*. Baton Rouge: Louisiana State University Press, revised edition, 1991.

————. *Race and Reunion: The Civil War in American Memory*. Cambridge: Belknap Press of Harvard University Press, 2001.

Campbell, Tunis G. *Sufferings of the Rev. T. G. Campbell and His Family, in Georgia*. Washington: Enterprise Publishing Company, 1877.

Cecelski, David S., ed. *Democracy Betrayed: The Wilmington Race Riot of 1898 and Its Legacy*. Chapel Hill: University of North Carolina Press, 1998.

————. *The Fire of Freedom: Abraham Galloway and the Slaves' Civil War*. Chapel Hill: University of North Carolina Press, 2012.

Chafe, William H., Raymond Gavins, and Robert Korstad, eds. *Remembering Jim Crow: African Americans Tell About Life in the Segregated South*. New York: The New Press, 2001.

Chernow, Ron. *Grant*. New York: Penguin Press, 2017.

Downs, Gregory P. *After Appomattox: Military Occupation and the Ends of War*. Cambridge: Harvard University Press, 2015.

Downs, Gregory P., and Kate Masur, eds. *The World the Civil War Made*. Chapel Hill: University of North Carolina Press, 2015.

Downs, Gregory P., and Scott Nesbit. *Mapping Occupation: Force, Freedom, and the Army in Reconstruction*, http://mappingoccupation.org, March 2015.

Dray, Philip. *Capitol Men: The Epic Story of Reconstruction through the Lives of the First Black Congressmen.* Boston: Houghton Mifflin Co., 2008.

Du Bois, W. E. B. *Black Reconstruction: An Essay Toward a History of the Part Which Black Folk Played in the Attempt to Reconstruct Democracy in America, 1860–1880,* with an introduction by David Levering Lewis, edited by Henry Louis Gates, Jr. New York: Oxford University Press, 2007.

———. *The Souls of Black Folk,* edited by Henry Louis Gates, Jr. New York: Oxford University Press, 2014.

Duncan, Russell. *Freedom's Shore: Tunis Campbell and the Georgia Freedmen.* Athens: University of Georgia Press, 1986.

Egerton, Douglas R. *Thunder at the Gates: The Black Civil War Regiments that Redeemed America.* New York: Basic Books, 2016.

———. *The Wars of Reconstruction: The Brief, Violent History of America's Most Progressive Era.* New York: Bloomsbury Press, 2014.

Faust, Drew Gilpin. *This Republic of Suffering: Death and the American Civil War.* New York: Vintage, 2009.

Fitzgerald, Michael W. *Reconstruction in Alabama: From Civil War to Redemption in the Cotton South.* Baton Rouge: Louisiana State University Press, 2017.

Fleming, Walter L. "'Pap' Singleton, the Moses of the Colored Exodus," *American Journal of Sociology,* July 1909, pp. 61–82.

Foner, Eric. *The Fiery Trial: Abraham Lincoln and American Slavery.* New York: W. W. Norton, 2011.

———. *Freedom's Lawmakers: A Directory of Black Officeholders during Reconstruction,* revised edition. Baton Rouge: Louisiana State University Press, 1996.

———. *Reconstruction: America's Unfinished Revolution, 1863–1877,* updated edition. New York: Harper Perennial, 2014.

Foner, Philip S., and Yuval Taylor, eds. *Frederick Douglass: Selected Speeches and Writings*. Chicago: Lawrence Hill Books, 1999. Kindle edition.

Foreman, Gabrielle P., Jim Casey, Sarah Lynn Patterson, co-founders. *Colored Conventions: Bringing Nineteenth-Century Black Organizing to Digital Life*, http://coloredconventions.org.

Franklin, John Hope, and Higginbotham, Evelyn Brooks. *From Slavery to Freedom: A History of African Americans*. 9th ed. New York: McGraw-Hill, 2011.

————. *Reconstruction after the Civil War*, 3rd edition, with a new foreword by Eric Foner. Chicago: University of Chicago Press, 2013.

Last Seen: Finding Family After Slavery. Villanova University Department of History, 2016–18. http://informationwanted.org.

Giddings, Paula J. *Ida: A Sword among Lions: Ida B. Wells and the Campaign against Lynching*. New York: Amistad, 2008.

Gienapp, William E., ed. *The Civil War and Reconstruction: A Documentary Collection*. New York: W. W. Norton, 2001.

Goodheart, Adam. *1861: The Civil War Awakening*. New York: Knopf, 2011.

Grimké, Charlotte L. Forten. *The Journals of Charlotte Forten Grimké*, edited by Brenda Stevenson. New York: Oxford University Press, 1989.

Guelzo, Allen C. *Reconstruction: A Concise History*. New York: Oxford University Press, 2018.

Hahn, Steven. *A Nation under Our Feet: Black Political Struggles in the Rural South from Slavery to the Great Migration*. Cambridge: Belknap Press of Harvard University, 2005.

————. *A Nation without Borders: The United States and Its World in an Age of Civil Wars, 1830–1910*. New York: Penguin, 2016.

Higginbotham, Evelyn Brooks. *Righteous Discontent: The Women's Movement in the Black Baptist Church, 1880–1920*. Cambridge: Harvard University Press, 1993.

Higginson, Thomas Wentworth, *Army Life in a Black Regiment.* Boston: Fields, Osgood & Co., 1870.

Holt, Thomas. *Black over White: Negro Political Leadership in South Carolina during Reconstruction.* Chicago: University of Illinois Press, 1979.

Holzer, Harold, Edna Greene Medford, and Frank J. Williams. *The Emancipation Proclamation: Three Views.* Baton Rouge: Louisiana State University Press, 2006.

Hunter, Tera W. *Bound in Wedlock: Slave and Free Black Marriage in the Nineteenth Century.* Cambridge and London: Belknap Press of Harvard University Press, 2017.

————. *To 'joy My Freedom: Southern Black Women's Lives and Labors after the Civil War.* Cambridge: Harvard University Press, 1997.

Lehr, Dick. *The Birth of a Movement: How Birth of a Nation Ignited the Battle for Civil Rights.* New York: PublicAffairs, 2017.

Library of Congress, *A Small Nation of People: W. E. B. Du Bois and African American Portraits of Progress,* with essays by David Levering Lewis and Deborah Willis. New York: Amistad, 2003.

Logan, Rayford W. *The Betrayal of the Negro: From Rutherford B. Hayes to Woodrow Wilson,* with a new introduction by Eric Foner. New York: Da Capo Press, 1997.

Lynch, John Roy. *The Facts of Reconstruction.* New York: The Neale Publishing Co., 1913.

————. *Reminiscences of an Active Life: The Autobiography of John Roy Lynch,* edited and with an introduction by John Hope Franklin. Jackson: University Press of Mississippi, 2008.

Merritt, Carole, ed. *Something So Horrible: The Springfield Race Riot of 1908.* Springfield: Abraham Lincoln Presidential Library Foundation, 2008, https://www.illinois.gov/alplm/museum/Education/Documents/Race_Riot_Catalog_2008.pdf.

Morris, Roy Jr. *Fraud of the Century: Rutherford B. Hayes, Samuel Tilden, and the Stolen Election of 1876.* New York: Simon & Schuster, 2004.

Painter, Nell Irvin. *Exodusters: Black Migration to Kansas after Reconstruction.* New York: W. W. Norton, 1992.

Perry, Imani. *May We Forever Stand: A History of the Black National Anthem.* Chapel Hill: University of North Carolina Press, 2018.

Peters, Gerhard, and John T. Woolley, eds. *The American Presidency Project*, http://www.presidency.ucsb.edu.

Rowland, Leslie S., project director. *Freedmen & Southern Society Project*, http://www.freedmen.umd.edu.

Siddali, Silvana R. *From Property to Person: Slavery and the Confiscation Acts, 1861–1862.* Baton Rouge: Louisiana State University Press, 2005.

Simpson, Brooks D. *Reconstruction: Voices from America's First Great Struggle for Racial Equality.* New York: Library of America, 2018.

———. *The Reconstruction Presidents.* Lawrence: University Press of Kansas, 1998.

Smith, John David. *Black Voices from Reconstruction, 1865–1877.* Gainesville: University Press of Florida, 1998.

Smock, Raymond W. *Booker T. Washington: Black Leadership in the Age of Jim Crow.* Library of African-American Biography. Chicago: Ivan R. Dee, 2009.

Sterling, Dorothy, ed. *The Trouble They Seen: The Story of Reconstruction in the Words of African Americans.* New York: Da Capo Press, 1994.

Sullivan, Patricia. *Lift Every Voice: The NAACP and the Making of the Civil Rights Movement.* New York: New Press, 2009.

Taylor, Susie King. *Reminiscences of My Life in Camp with the 33d United States Colored Troops Late 1st S. C. Volunteers.* Boston: self-published, 1902.

Trefousse, Hans L. *Andrew Johnson: A Biography.* New York: W. W. Norton, 1997.

————. *Historical Dictionary of Reconstruction*. Westport, CT: Greenwood Press, 1991.

Troxler, Carole Watterson. "'To look more closely at the man': Wyatt Outlaw, a Nexus of National, Local, and Personal History," *North Carolina Historical Review*, October 2000, pp. 403–433.

Washington, Booker T. *Up from Slavery: An Autobiography*. Garden City, NY: Doubleday and Co., 1901.

White, Richard. *The Republic for Which It Stands: The United States during Reconstruction and the Gilded Age, 1865–1896*. New York: Oxford University Press, 2017.

Williams, David. *I Freed Myself: African American Self-Emancipation in the Civil War*. New York: Cambridge University Press, 2014.

Williams, Heather Andrea. *Help Me to Find My People: The African American Search for Family Lost in Slavery*. John Hope Franklin Series in African American History and Culture. Chapel Hill: University of North Carolina Press, 2012.

Williams, Kidada E. *They Left Great Marks on Me: African American Testimonies of Racial Violence from Emancipation to World War I*. New York University Press, 2012.

Woodward, C. Vann. *The Strange Career of Jim Crow*, commemorative edition with an afterword by William S. McFeely. New York: Oxford University Press, 2002.

Source Notes

1 LET FREEDOM RING!

"My Country 'Tis of Thee": https://kids.niehs.nih.gov/games/songs/patriotic/my-country-tis-of-thee/index.htm.

"I motioned them . . . unloosed": Thomas Wentworth Higginson, *Army Life in a Black Regiment* (Boston: Fields, Osgood & Co., 1870), p. 41.

"the trump of jubilee": Frederick Douglass, *Life and Times of Frederick Douglass* (Hartford, CT: Park Publishing, 1882), p. 429.

"On the 1st of January, 1863 . . .": Susie King Taylor, *Reminiscences of My Life in Camp with the 33d United States Colored Troops Late 1st S. C. Volunteers* (Boston: self-published, 1902), p. 18.

"the most eventful day . . . honesty of her intention": "Letter from Dr. Seth Rogers to wife Hannah Mitchell Rogers, January 1, 1863," in Matthew Pinsker, "Emancipation Among Black Troops in South Carolina," November 6, 2012, http://housedivided.dickinson.edu/sites/emancipation/2012/11/06/emancipation-among-black-troops-in-south-carolina.

"Just think of it! . . . unknown people's song": Thomas Wentworth Higginson, *Army Life*, p. 41.

Prince Rivers's physical description: USCT Enlistment card, in Matthew Pinsker, "General Hunter 'Confiscates' Prince Rivers, November 8, 2012, http://housedivided.dickinson.edu/sites/emancipation/2012/11/08/general-hunter-confiscates-prince-rivers.

"There is not a white officer . . .": Thomas Wentworth Higginson, "An Officer on the Colored Soldiers," *Liberator*, February 24, 1865, p. 32.

"I am under no constitutional . . ." and "contraband of war . . .": T. A. Bland, *Life of Benjamin F. Butler* (Boston: Lee and Shepard, 1879), p. 52.

"Though I was a mere child . . .": Booker T. Washington, *Up from Slavery: An Autobiography* (Garden City, NY: Doubleday & Co., 1901), pp. 7–8.

on the number of people who escaped to Fort Monroe within days of Butler's decree: Henry Louis Gates Jr. "The Black Roots of Memorial Day," May 26, 2014, http://www.theroot.com/the-black-roots-of-memorial-day-1790875788.

"Up to this time . . . of the non-laborers": "Commander of the Department of Virginia to the General-in-Chief of the Army," Freedmen & Southern Society Project, http://www.freedmen.umd.edu/Butler.html.

"Within weeks . . . *were* Union lines": Adam Goodheart, *1861: The Civil War Awakening* (New York: Knopf, 2011), p. 341.

"shapely head . . . for the imperial review" and "meanest man": John W. Blassingame, ed., "Harry Jarvis," *Slave Testimony: Two Centuries of Letters, Speech, Interviews, and Autobiographies* (Baton Rouge: Louisiana State University Press, 1977), p. 607.

"a black man's war" and "*would* be a black man's war before they got through." John W. Blassingame, ed., "Harry Jarvis," *Slave Testimony*, p. 608. The second quotation has been silently corrected for readability.

On Jarvis's travels: Douglas R. Egerton, *Thunder at the Gates: The Black Civil War Regiments that Redeemed America* (New York: Basic Books, 2016), p. 42.

"captives of war . . .": "The Second Confiscation Act," Freedmen & Southern Society Project, http://www.freedmen.umd.edu/conact2.htm.

"ten dollars per month . . .": "Details of the Militia Act of 1862," Freedmen & Southern Society Project, http://www.freedmen.umd.edu/milact.htm.

"a fit and necessary war measure": "Transcript of Emancipation Proclamation (1863)," Our Documents, https://www.ourdocuments.gov/doc.php?flash=false&doc=34&page=transcript.

"Hurrah!": Susie King Taylor, *Reminiscences of My Life*, p. 18.

"in forming a Confederacy of Slaveholding States": "Address of South Carolina to Slaveholding States," December 25, 1860, http://teachingamericanhistory.org/library/document/address-of-south-carolina-to-slaveholding-states.

2 MEN OF COLOR TO ARMS!

"The national edifice is on fire . . . rules the hour": "Fighting Rebels with Only One Hand," *Douglass' Monthly*, September 1861, p. 516.

"a class of people not fit to govern themselves": David S. Cecelski, *The Fire of Freedom: Abraham Galloway and the Slaves' Civil War* (Chapel Hill: University of North Carolina Press, 2012), p. xviii.

"Now the main question is . . .": Ira Berlin, Joseph P. Reidy, and Leslie S. Rowland, eds., *Freedom's Soldiers: The Black Military Experience in the Civil War* (New York: Cambridge University Press, 1998), pp. 114–115.

"There I was wounded . . .": John W. Blassingame, ed., "Harry Jarvis," *Slave Testimony*, p. 609. The quotation has been silently corrected for readability.

On Jarvis's wounding in battle: The official army paperwork puts Jarvis at the November 1864 Battle of Honey Hill. When interviewed in 1872 Jarvis said he was wounded at the Battle of Folly Island (John W. Blassingame, ed., "Harry Jarvis," *Slave Testimony*, p. 609). That battle occurred in May 1863, months before Jarvis enlisted. In a footnote to the entry on Jarvis, Blassingame's *Slave Testimony* (page 609) states that Jarvis "joined the regiment at Folly Island on January 18, 1864. His leg was fractured at Honey Hill, South Carolina, on November 30, 1864."

"I have received your last kind letter . . .": "Missouri Slave Woman to Her Soldier Husband," Freedmen & Southern Society Project, http://www.freedmen.umd.edu/Glover.html.

"First night's sleep since 27th": "Diary of Sergeant Major Christian A. Fleetwood U.S. Colored Infantry Fourth Regiment, Company G, 1864 Excerpts," http://nationalhumanitiescenter.org/pds/maai/identity/text7/fleetwooddiary.pdf.

"We are in winter quarters . . .": Diana Penner, "Black Soldier's Letter Offers Rare View of Civil War," *Indianapolis Star*, March 4, 2013, https://www.usatoday.com/story/news/nation/2013/03/04/black-soldier-civil-war-letter-auction/1962533.

number of black people who served in the Union army and navy: "Black Soldiers in the U.S. Military During the Civil War," National Archives, https://www.archives.gov/education/lessons/blacks-civil-war.

number of black people who escaped to Union lines: "Contraband of War," National Park Service, https://www.nps.gov/parkhistory/online_books/civil_war_series/2/sec4.htm.

military and civilian deaths: Richard White, *The Republic for Which It Stands: The United States During Reconstruction and the Gilded Age, 1865–1896* (New York: Oxford University Press, 2017), p. 28 and Rachel Coker, "Historian Revises Estimate of Civil War Dead," Discover-e Binghamton Research, September 21, 2011, https://discovere.binghamton.edu/news /civilwar-3826.html.

3 FRAUGHT WITH GREAT DIFFICULTY

Abraham Lincoln's Proclamation of Amnesty and Reconstruction: Freedmen & Southern Society Project, http://www.freedmen.umd.edu/procamn.htm.

"Is it not madness . . . provide for the execution:" James F. Wilson, *A Free Constitution: Speech of Hon. James F. Wilson, of Iowa* (W.H. Moore, printer, 1864), p. 16.

"Neither slavery nor involuntary servitude . . .": "Transcript of 13th Amendment to the U.S. Constitution: Abolition of Slavery (1865)," Our Documents, https://www .ourdocuments.gov/doc.php?flash=false&doc=40&page=transcript.

"Christmas gift": "President Lincoln's Christmas Gift, 1864," The White House Historical Association, https://www.whitehousehistory.org/president-lincolns-christmas-gift-1864.

Sherman and Stanton's meeting the black clerics: Ira Berlin, Joseph P. Reidy, and Leslie S. Rowland, "Minutes of an Interview Between the Colored Ministers and Church Officers at Savannah with the Secretary of War and Major-Gen. Sherman," *Freedom's Soldiers: The Black Military Experience in the Civil War* (New York: Cambridge University Press, 1998), p. 149–53.

'What course can be clearer . . .": "What Shall Be Done with the Slaves?" *Weekly Anglo-African*, November 23, 1861, p. 2.

"It seems to me, General, . . . no law here except mine, Mr. Secretary": Frank Abial Flower, *Edwin McMasters Stanton: The Autocrat of Rebellion, Emancipation, and Reconstruction* (Akron, OH: Saalfield Publishing Co, 1905), p. 298.

"The pews, in the body of the house . . . corn and cotton": "Meeting of the Freedmen," *Savannah Daily Herald*, February 3, 1865, p. 2.

"Some months ago I complained . . .": Dorothy Sterling, ed., *The Trouble They Seen: The Story of Reconstruction in the Words of African Americans* (New York: Da Capo Press, 1994), p. 68.

"We left with rations . . .": Dorothy Sterling, ed., *The Trouble They Seen*, p. 34.

Lincoln's last speech: "Last Public Address," Abraham Lincoln Online, http://www .abrahamlincolnonline.org/lincoln/speeches/last.htm.

"Outside was a vast . . . surprised, multitude": Noah Brooks, *Washington in Lincoln's Time* (New York: The Century Co., 1896), p. 255.

"That is the last speech he will ever make": Vernon Burton, "Lincoln's Last Speech," May 2009, http://www.las.illinois.edu/news/lincoln/lastspeech.

Andrew Johnson's address in Nashville: "October 24, 1864," last updated April 14, 2015, https://www.nps.gov/anjo/learn/historyculture/moses-speech.htm.

"treason must be . . .": Brooks D. Simpson, *The Reconstruction Presidents*, p. 68.

4 RESTORED

Andrew Johnson's Proclamation 134: The American Presidency Project, http://www
.presidency.ucsb.edu/ws/index.php?pid=72392.

Andrew Johnson's Proclamation 135: The American Presidency Project, http://www
.presidency.ucsb.edu/ws/index.php?pid=72403.

"General, there is no such thing . . . protection of the Union": Paul II. Bergeron, ed., *The
Papers of Andrew Johnson*, volume 8, May–August 1865 (Knoxville: University of
Tennessee Press, 1989), p. 154.

"Well, the war is over . . .": "The Late Convention of Colored Men," *New York Times*, August
13, 1865. http://www.nytimes.com/1865/08/13/news/late-convention-colored-men
-address-loyal-citizens-united-states-congress.html?pagewanted=all.

"We the freedmen of Edisto Island . . .": "Committee of Freedmen on Edisto Island,
South Carolina, to the Freedmen's Bureau Commissioner; the Commissioner's Reply; and
the Committee to the President," http://www.freedmen.umd.edu/Edisto%20petitions.htm.

On Dinah Greeen, Ned Richardson, and Titus Neal: "Register of Land Titles Issued to
Freedmen," Freedmen's Bureau Online, http://freedmensbureau.com/georgia/landtitles
/georgialand3.htm.

"All persons of color . . .": "South Carolina's 'Black Codes,'" Lowcountry Digital History
Initiative, http://ldhi.library.cofc.edu/exhibits/show/after_slavery_educator/unit_three
_documents/document_eight.

Mississippi's Black Codes: "Black Codes of Mississippi, TeachingAmericanHistory.org,
http://teachingamericanhistory.org/library/document/black-codes-of-mississippi.

On Florida's black codes allowing for black people to be whipped and pilloried: Codes:
T. D. Allman, Finding Florida: The True History of the Sunshine State (Atlantic Monthly
Press, 2013), p. 252.

"When the war closed . . .": M. F. Armstrong and Helen W. Ludlow. *Hampton and Its Students
by Two of Its Teachers* (New York: G.P. Putnam's Sons, 1903), pp. 79–80.

"About the 4th of August 1865 . . .": "Freedmen's Bureau List of Outrages Perpetrated by
the Whites Upon The Freedmen in the State of Tennessee from April 1865 to March
1866," Freedmen's Bureau Online, http://www.freedmensbureau.com/tennessee/outrages
/tennoutrages1.htm.

"into the fire place . . .": "Freedmen's Bureau Report of Murders and Outrages in Texas,"
Freedmen's Bureau Online, http://www.freedmensbureau.com/texas/texasoutrages3.htm.

on woman thrown from trolley car: "Assaults," Freedmen's Bureau Online, http://www
.freedmensbureau.com/washingtondc/outrages2.htm.

"The revolutionary schemes . . . recently in rebellion": "Negro Government or Disunion,"
Daily Milwaukee News, December 5, 1865, p. 4.

"Is there no way to arrest . . .": Hans L. Trefousse, *Andrew Johnson: A Biography* (New
York: W.W. Norton, 1989), p. 217.

"Dead men cannot raise . . .": Beverly Wilson Palmer and Holly Byers Ochoa, eds.,
"Reconstruction, December 18, 1865, in Congress," *The Selected Papers of Thaddeus
Stevens*, volume 2: April 1865–August 1868 (Pittsburgh: University of Pittsburgh Press,
1998), p. 45.

"If we leave them to the legislation . . .": Beverly Wilson Palmer and Holly Byers Ochoa,
eds., "Reconstruction, December 18, 1865, in Congress," *The Selected Papers of Thaddeus*

Stevens, volume 2: April 1865–August 1868 (Pittsburgh: University of Pittsburgh Press, 1997), p. 52.

Isaac Williams's ad: "Isaac Williams offers $200 reward to anyone who can find his grandson," Reward Ad, *South Carolina Leader* (Charleston), December 09, 1865, Last Seen: Finding Family After Slavery, accessed September 9, 2017, http://informationwanted.org /items/show/2164.

The Vinsons' ad: "Peter Vinson and Peggy Vinson searching for their daughter," Information Wanted Ad, *Tri-Weekly Standard* (Raleigh, NC), May 31, 1866, *Last Seen: Finding Family After Slavery*, accessed September 9, 2017, http://informationwanted.org/items /show/2743.

Buckner's ad: "Robert Buckner," Information Wanted Ad, *The Christian Recorder* (Philadelphia, PA), First Ad: February 2nd, 1867, *Last Seen: Finding Family After Slavery*, accessed September 9, 2017, http://informationwanted.org/items/show/240.

Curren's ad: "Mollie Curren (nee Agnes Thorp?) searching for her aunts and uncle," Information Wanted Ad, *Richmond Planet* (Richmond, VA), October 5, 1907, *Last Seen: Finding Family After Slavery*, accessed September 9, 2017, http://informationwanted.org /items/show/2754.

5 THE BALLOT WITH WHICH TO SAVE OURSELVES

on black conventions: "Colored Conventions," http://coloredconventions.org/conventions.

"We are engaged in a serious task . . . rights as men": *State Convention of Colored Men of the State of Tennessee, Proceedings of the State Convention of Colored Men of the State of Tennessee* (Nashville: Daily Press and Times Job Office, 1865), pp. 7–8.

"the ballot with . . . in saving the nation:" "Interview with a Colored Delegation Respecting Suffrage," in Edward McPherson, *A Political Manual for 1866* (Washington, DC: Philp & Solomons, 1866), p. 52.

"Yes, I have said, and I repeat here . . . of his blood": "Interview with a Colored Delegation Respecting Suffrage," in Edward McPherson, *A Political Manual for 1866* (Washington, DC: Philp & Solomons, 1866), p. 53.

catechism: Dorothy Sterling, ed., *The Trouble They Seen*, p. 28.

Fourteenth Amendment: "Transcript of 14th Amendment to the U.S. Constitution: Civil Rights (1868)," https://www.ourdocuments.gov/doc.php?flash=false&doc=43&page =transcript.

"Large sums of [black people's] money . . . burn up the cradle": "The Freedmen's Bureau Report on the Memphis Race Riots of 1866," http://teachingamericanhistory.org/library /document/the-freedmens-bureau-report-on-the-memphis-race-riots-of-1866.

Lavinia Goodell's testimony: United States Congress, House Select Committee on the Memphis Riots. *Memphis Riots and Massacres* (Washington, DC: Government Printing Office, 1866), pp. 78–79.

"to secure, by political and moral means . . .": *Minutes of the Freedmen's Convention, Held in the City of Raleigh, on the 2nd, 3rd, 4th and 5th of October, 1866* (Raleigh: Standard Book and Job Office, 1866, p. 27.

"It is a large three-story brick building . . . school purposes": Dorothy Sterling, ed., *The Trouble They Seen*, p. 13.

6 GO ON WITH YOUR OPPRESSIONS

"I am for negro suffrage . . . they deserve it": Beverly Wilson Palmer and Holly Byers Ochoa, eds., "Reconstruction," *The Selected Papers of Thaddeus Stevens*, volume 2: April 1865–August 1868 (Pittsburgh: University of Pittsburgh Press, 1998), p. 220.

on troop strength in the military districts: David Vergun, "150 years ago: Army Takes on Peacekeeping Duties in post-Civil War South," August 3, 2015, https://www.army.mil /article/153230/150_years_ago_army_takes_on_peacekeeping_duties_in_post_civil _war_south.

Alabama's black population in 1860: "Results from the 1860 Census," The Civil War Home Page, http://www.civil-war.net/pages/1860_census.html.

delegates at Alabama's convention: "This Week in Alabama History," Alabama Department of Archives and History," http://www.archives.alabama.gov/thisweek /month.html.

delegates at Georgia's convention: William Harris Bragg, "Reconstruction in Georgia," 10/21/2005, last edited by NGE Staff on 10/19/2016, New Georgia Encyclopedia, https:// www.georgiaencyclopedia.org/articles/history-archaeology/reconstruction-georgia.

Georgia's black population in 1860: "Results from the 1860 Census," The Civil War Home Page, http://www.civil-war.net/pages/1860_census.html.

delegates at South Carolina's convention: Hyman S. Rubin III, "Reconstruction," SC Encyclopedia, http://www.scencyclopedia.org/sce/entries/reconstruction.

South Carolina's black population in 1860: "Results from the 1860 Census," The Civil War Home Page, http://www.civil-war.net/pages/1860_census.html.

"a most remarkable group . . . political power center": Col. Samuel Taylor, "Reconstruction Georgia, Georgia History 101, Our Georgia History, http://www .ourgeorgiahistory.com/history101/gahistory08.html.

"I remarked in a former letter . . . what they say": "South Carolina," *New York Times*, January 21, 1868, p. 2.

South Carolina's new state constitution: "Constitution of the State of South Carolina, 1868," Teaching American History in South Carolina, http://www.teachingushistory.org /ttrove/1868Constitution.htm.

estimated number of black officeholders during Reconstruction: Eric Foner, "Rooted in Reconstruction: The First Wave of Black Congressmen," the Nation, October 15, 2008, https://www.thenation.com/article/rooted-reconstruction-first-wave-black-congressmen.

"their fair complexion . . .": John Hope Franklin, Reconstruction after the Civil War, 3rd. edition, (Chicago: University of Chicago Press, 2013), p. 130.

"Go on with your oppressions . . .": Andre E. Johnson, *The Forgotten Prophet: Bishop Henry McNeal Turner and the African American Prophetic Tradition* (Lanham, MD: Lexington Books, 2012), p. 65.

"killing about a dozen and wounding possibly thirty others," Lee W. Formwalt, "Camilla Massacre," September 5, 2002, last edited by NGE Staff on August 1, 2016, *New Georgia /Encyclopedia*, http://m.georgiaencyclopedia.org/articles/history-archaeology/ camilla-massacre.

"Oh Daddy, Oh daddy! and "Beware! Ye guilty parties—both white and black": Walter Boyd. "The Life and Tragic Death of Wyatt Outlaw," *Times-News*, August 16, 2015, http:// www.thetimesnews.com/article/20150816/NEWS/150819177.

on Outlaw being a widower: Ancestry.com. U.S. Federal Census Mortality Schedules, 1850–1885 [database online]. Provo, UT, USA: Ancestry.com Operations, Inc., 2010.

"Transcript of 15th Amendment to the U.S. Constitution: Voting Rights (1870), Our Documents, https://www.ourdocuments.gov/doc.php?flash=false&doc=44&page =transcript.

"the right by which all others could be secured": Waldo E. Martin, *The Mind of Frederick Douglass* (Chapel Hill, NC: University of North Carolina Press, 1984), p. 147.

"News of the failure to convict Johnson . . .": Hans L. Trefousse, *Andrew Johnson: A Biography* (New York: W.W. Norton, 1989), p. 333.

7 WHITE REIGN OF TERROR

"The Ku-Klux Conspiracy": Eugene Lawrence, "The Ku-Klux Conspiracy," October 19, 1872, *Harper's Weekly*, p. 805.

"the first presidential election where . . .": Brooks D. Simpson, "The Election of 1868," April 1, 2011, https://cwcrossroads.wordpress.com/2011/04/01/the-election-of-1868.

"and sixty-five ringleaders . . .": Jean Edward Smith, "Crushing the Klan" (Letter to the Editor), *New York Times*, June 10, 2001, http://www.nytimes.com/2001/06/10/books/l -crushing-the-klan-579572.html.

"When myself and my colleagues . . .": "Rainey, Joseph Hayne," History, Art & Archives, United States House of Representatives, http://history.house.gov/People/Listing/R /RAINEY,-Joseph-Hayne-(R000016).

"The total number killed . . . anonymous graves": Richard White, *The Republic for Which It Stands: The United States During Reconstruction and the Gilded Age, 1865– 1896* (New York: Oxford University Press, 2017), pp. 279–80.

Inscription on Colfax monument: Richard Rubin, "The Colfax Riot," the *Atlantic*, July /August 2003, https://www.theatlantic.com/magazine/archive/2003/07/the-colfax-riot /378556.

"A White Reign of Terror in Louisiana": New York Herald, September 3, 1874, p. 4.

"The Vicksburg Riot": *Owyhee Daily Avalanche*, p. 2.

"For another ten days . . . wounded and terrorized": Steven Hahn, *A Nation under Our Feet: Black Political Struggles in the Rural South from Slavery to the Great Migration* (Massachusetts: Belknap Press of Harvard University, 2005), p. 298.

"Race Feuds in Mississippi": *New York Evening Post*, September 7, 1875, p. 4.

"just hunted . . . the same as birds": Melissa Janczewski Jone, "The Clinton Riot of 1875: From Riot to Massacre," http://www.mshistorynow.mdah.ms.gov/articles/399/ the-clinton-riot-of-1875-from-riot-to-massacre.

"Don't let the bill fail": "Landmark Legislation: Civil Rights Act of 1875," https://www .senate.gov/artandhistory/history/common/generic/CivilRightsAct1875.htm.

"I appeal to all the members . . . home of the brave' ": John Hope Franklin, ed., *Reminiscences of an Active Life: The Autobiography of John Roy Lynch* (Jackson: University Press of Mississippi 2008) p. xviii.

Exchange between Getsen and Adams: "The Hamburg Massacre," CSI: Dixie, https://csidixie.org/chronicles/hamburg-massacre.

"The effects of the massacre . . .": Richard Zuczek, "Hamburg Massacre," *SC Encyclopedia*, http://www.scencyclopedia.org/sce/entries/hamburg-massacre.

"On or about the 12th of January, 1876 . . . or a buggy trace": T. G. Campbell, *Sufferings of the Rev. T. G. Campbell and His Family, in Georgia* (Washington: Enterprise Publishing Company, 1877), p. 25.

on the Freedman's Bank: "Freedman's Savings & Trust Co.," White House Historical Association, https://www.whitehousehistory.org/freedmans-savings-trust-co.

8 TO THE STORM, TO THE WHIRLWIND

"to consider a policy that . . .": Ari Hoogenboom, "Rutherford B. Hayes and African-Americans," https://www.rbhayes.org/hayes/rutherford-b.-hayes-and-african-americans-by-ari-hoogenboom.

"You say you have emancipated us . . .: Frederick Douglass, "Speech of Mr. Douglass," in *Official Proceedings of the National Republican Conventions of 1868, 1872, 1876 and 1880* (Minneapolis, MN: Charles W. Johnson, 1903) p. 251.

"As the 7th of November . . . candidates of both parties": Quoted in "Betting," *Cleveland Daily Plain Dealer*, November 2, 1876, p. 1.

Providence Evening Press prediction: "The Presidential Contest," *Providence Evening Press*, November 8, 1876, p. 1.

"Not Yet, Sammy": *Inter Ocean*, November 9, 1876, p. 1.

"We have got through . . .": Charles Richard Williams, *The Life of Rutherford Birchard Hayes, Nineteenth President of the United States*, vol. 2 (Boston: Houghton Mifflin, 1914), p. 64.

"If war among the Whites. . . .": Julius E. Thompson , James L. Conyers Jr., and Nancy J. Dawson, eds., *The Frederick Douglass Encyclopedia* (Santa Barbara, CA: Greenwood Press, 2010), p. 114.

9 MORAL WEAKNESS IN HIGH PLACES

"The exodus . . . is altogether favorable": Logan, Rayford W. *The Betrayal of the Negro: From Rutherford B. Hayes to Woodrow Wilson* (New York: Da Capo Press, 1997), p. 32.

"full quick eyes": Walter L. Fleming, "'Pap' Singleton, the Moses of the Colored Exodus," *American Journal of Sociology*, July 1909, pp. 61–2.

"The Land That Gives Birth to Freedom" and "abundant room . . . for loafers": Walter L. Fleming, 'Pap' Singleton, the Moses of the Colored Exodus," *American Journal of Sociology*, July 1909, p. 67 and 66.

"The white people in Louisiana . . .": Darlene Clark Hine and Kathleen Thompson, *A Shining Thread of Hope: The History of Black Women in America* (New York: Broadway Books, 1999), p. 167.

"In the spring of 1879 . . . honest compensation": "Exodus to Kansas: The 1880 Senate Investigation of the Beginnings of the African American Migration from the South," *Prologue Magazine*, Summer 2008, https://www.archives.gov/publications/prologue/2008/summer/exodus.html.

"it was utterly impossible to live . . .": Steven Hahn, *A Nation under Our Feet*, p. 319.

Adams's fact-finding mission: Dorothy Sterling, ed., *The Trouble They Seen*, p. 271, 273.

"Not only is the South the best locality . . .": "The Negro Exodus from the Gulf States," *Journal of Social Science,* May 1880, p. 18.

"out of a passion . . . rather than preparation": Nell Irvin Painter, *Exodusters: Black Migration to Kansas After Reconstruction* (New York: W. W. Norton & Company, 1992), p. 243.

Kansas's black population 1870–1880: Todd Arrington, "Exodusters, National Park Service, https://www.nps.gov/home/learn/historyculture/exodusters.htm.

sharecropping percentages in Mississippi: "Sharecropping in Mississippi," the *American Experience,* http://www.pbs.org/wgbh/americanexperience/features/emmett-sharecropping -mississippi.

"the turn of the twentieth century . . .": Steven Hahn, *A Nation under Our Feet,* p. 457.

"We feel it, as we felt . . . slavery from the beginning": Frederick Douglass, "Speech at the Civil Rights Mass-Meeting Held at Lincoln Hall, October 22, 1883," http:// teachingamericanhistory.org/library/document/the-civil-rights-case.

"We came here to exclude the Negro": Neil R. McMillen, "Isaiah T. Montgomery, 1847-1924 (Part II)," Mississippi History Now, http://www.mshistorynow.mdah.ms.gov /articles/57/isaiah-t-montgomery-1847-1924-part-ii.

Mississippi's black population: Jordan Malone, "The Voting History of Mississippi: The Convention of 1890," Mississippi Votes, https://www.msvotes.org/single-post/2017/11/20 /The-Voting-History-of-Mississippi-The-Convention-of-1890.

on black registered voters in Mississippi: "White Only: Jim Crow in America," http:// americanhistory.si.edu/brown/history/1-segregated/white-only-1.html.

"But Barrett took the altercation . . . for maintaining a public nuisance": Mia Bay, *To Tell the Truth Freely: The Life of Ida B. Wells* (New York: Hill & Wang, 2010), Kindle.

"a desolate field just . . . covered with some brush": Mia Bay, *To Tell the Truth Freely: The Life of Ida B. Wells* (New York: Hill & Wang, 2010), Kindle.

"O God . . . no peace, no justice in this land for us?": Miriam DeCosta-Willis, ed., *The Memphis Diary of Ida B. Wells: An Intimate Portrait of the Activist as a Young Woman* (Boston: Beacon Press, 1995), p. 141.

"In slave times the Negro . . . execution": Ida B. Wells, *The Red Record: Tabulated Statistics and Alleged Causes of Lynching in the United States* (1895), p. 1.

black population in 1890: Campbell Gibson and Kay Jung, "Table A-1. Race and Hispanic Origin for the United States: 1790 to 1990," Historical Census Statistics On Population Totals By Race, 1790 to 1990, and By Hispanic Origin, 1970 to 1990, For Large Cities And Other Urban Places In The United States (Washington, DC: U.S. Census Bureau, February 1995).

"These companies . . . convicts are Negroes": *The Reason Why the Colored American Is Not in the World's Columbian Exposition* (Chicago: n.p., 1893), p. 19.

Washington's Atlanta Expo speech: "Booker T. Washington Delivers the 1895 Atlanta Compromise Speech," History Matters, George Mason University, http://historymatters .gmu.edu/d/39.

"equal but separate accommodations . . .": "Separate but Equal: The Law of the Land," http://americanhistory.si.edu/brown/history/1-segregated/separate-but-equal.html.

"We consider the underlying . . . construction upon it": "Plessy v. Ferguson," Legal Information Institute, Cornell Law School, https://www.law.cornell.edu/supremecourt /text/163/537.

"Our Constitution is color-blind . . . amendments to the Constitution": "Plessy v. Ferguson," Legal Information Institute, Cornell Law School, https://www.law.cornell.edu /supremecourt/text/163/537.

10 MIGHTY CURRENT

"We Specialize in the Wholly Impossible": Darlene Clark Hine, Wilma King, and Linda Reed, eds., *We Specialize in the Wholly Impossible: A Reader in Black Women's History* (New York: NYU Press, 1995), p. iv.

"the largest negro population . . .": Thomas J. Calloway, "The Negro Exhibit" in *Report of the Commissioner-General for the United States to the International Universal Exposition, Paris, 1900*, vol 2. (Washington, DC: Government Printing Office, 1901), p. 465.

"To the Paris Exposition . . .": Eugene F. Jr. Provenzo, *W. E. B. DuBois's Exhibit of American Negroes: African Americans at the Beginning of the Twentieth Century* (Lanham, MD: Rowman and Littlefield, 2013), p. xi.

"an honest, straightforward . . .": The Library of Congress, *A Small Nation of People: W E. B. Du Bois and African American Portraits of Progress* (New York: Amistad/HarperCollins, 2003), p. 18.

"Lift Every Voice and Sing": "Lift Every Voice and Sing," Black Culture Connection," PBS, http://www.pbs.org/black-culture/explore/black-authors-spoken-word-poetry /lift-every-voice-and-sing.

"The onslaught of white supremacy . . .": "White, George Henry," History, Art & Archives, United States House of Representatives, http://history.house.gov/People/Detail?id=23657.

"This, Mr. Chairman, is . . . rising people, full of potential force." *Defense of the Negro Race—Charges Answered. Speech of Hon. George H. White, of North Carolina, in the House of Representatives, January 29, 1901* (Washington, DC, n.p., 1901), p. 14.

"self–sufficient blacks . . .": "White, George Henry," History, Art & Archives, United States House of Representatives, http://history.house.gov/People/Detail?id=23657.

"For Every Right, with All Thy Might": Dick Lehr, *The Birth of a Movement: How Birth of a Nation Ignited the Battle for Civil Rights* (New York: Public Affairs, 2017). Kindle edition.

"mighty current": Special Collections Archives, CREDO, Is Online, University of Massachusetts at Amherst press release, July 12, 2011, https://www.umass.edu /newsoffice/article/special-collections-archives-credo-online.

"Resolved, . . .": *An Open Letter to College Men: The Meaning of the Niagara Movement and the Junior Niagara Movement*, c. 1906, p. 7, Special collections and University Archives, University of Massachusetts Amherst, http://credo.library.umass.edu/view/full/ mums312-b004-i219.

"The eastern sky is lurid with the reflection of raging fires": Carole Merritt, *Something So Horrible: The Springfield Race Riot of 1908* (Springfield: Abraham Lincoln Presidential Library Foundation, 2002), p. 32, https://www.illinois.gov/alplm/museum/Education/Documents /Race_Riot_Catalog_2008.pdf.

"Lincoln freed you . . . burn and murder": William English Walling, "The Race War in the North," the *Independent*, September 3, 1908, p. 529.

"Yet who realizes . . .": William English Walling, "The Race War in the North," the *Independent*, September 3, 1908, p. 534.

"set forth those facts . . .": W.E.B. DuBois, Editorial, *Crisis*, November 1910, p. 10.

"a splendid production": Cooper, John Milton, Jr., *Reconsidering Woodrow Wilson: Progressivism, Internationalism, War, and Peace.* (Baltimore: Johns Hopkins University Press, 2008) p. 121.

"Sir, you have now . . . alert and hopeful": Du Bois, W.E.B., "Another Open Letter to Woodrow Wilson," *Crisis*, September 1913, http://teachingamericanhistory.org/library /document/another-open-letter-to-woodrow-wilson.

"We have a wonderful history . . . 'Who are you anyway?'": Barbara Krauthhamer and Chad Williams, eds. *Major Problems in African American History*, 2d edition (Boston: Cenage Learning, 2018), p. 4.

"The exposition takes the negro . . . to 30.5 per cent": "Lincoln Jubilee to Open Today in the Coliseum," *Chicago Tribune*, August 22, 1915, p. 9.

On displays at Lincoln Jubilee: John H. Ballard, *Lincoln Jubilee Album: 50th Anniversary of Our Emancipation, Held in Chicago August 22d to September 16th, 1915* (Chicago: n.p., 1915) and Mabel O.Wilson, *Negro Building: Black Americans in the World of Fairs and Museums* (Berkeley: University of California Press, 2012).

"The crowning . . . dancers to their homes": "The Lincoln Jubilee and Fifty Years of Freedom Celebration Is Now Running at Full Blast at the Coliseum and Will Continue Each Day Until September 16th," *Broad Ax*, August 28, 1915, p. 1.

Photo Credits

JACKET

Cover photos ©: Paul Mobley; background: pashabo/Shutterstock.

INTERIOR

Photos ©: cover: Paul Mobley; cover background: pashabo/Shutterstock; x, xi, 3, 5, 10 top and bottom, 14, 22: Library of Congress; 25: 201Collection of the Smithsonian National Museum of African American History and Culture; 26, 28: Library of Congress; 31 top left: National Museum of American History, Smithsonian Institution; 31 top right: Library of Congress; 31 bottom left: National Archives and Records Administration; 32: Library of Congress; 34: Everett Historical/Shutterstock; 37: Fotosearch/ Getty Images; 38: Library of Congress; 42: Everett Historical/Shutterstock; 44, 47, 50: Library of Congress; 54: Moorland-Spingarn Research Center; 56, 59, 62, 71, 82, 83: Library of Congress; 88-89: Library of Congress/Getty Images; 94-95, 96, 99, 100, 104, 110: Library of Congress; 114: Hulton

Index

Note: Page numbers in *italics* refer to illustrations. Numbered military units can be found at the beginning of the index.

About the
Authors

Professor Henry Louis Gates, Jr., is the Alphonse Fletcher University Professor and Director of the Hutchins Center for African and African American Research at Harvard. He is an acclaimed author and critic who has unearthed literary gems. He also has produced, written, and hosted an array of documentary films for public television, including *Africa's Great Civilizations, Finding Your Roots, Black America Since MLK: And Still I Rise,* and *The African Americans: Many Rivers to Cross.* Gates is the recipient of fifty-five honorary degrees and numerous prizes. A member of the first class awarded "genius grants" by the MacArthur Foundation in 1981, he was, in 1998, the first African American scholar to be awarded the National Humanities Medal. In addition, he was named to *Time*'s "25 Most Influential Americans" list in 1997, *Ebony*'s "Power 150" list in 2009, and *Ebony*'s "Power 100" list in 2010 and 2012.

Tonya Bolden is the award-winning author of many notable books for children and young adults, among them the Coretta Scott King Author Honor–winning *Maritcha: A Nineteenth-Century American Girl*, which was also a James Madison Book Award Winner and CCBC Best Book of the Year. Ms. Bolden's *Emancipation Proclamation: Lincoln and the Dawn of Liberty* was named a Bank Street College of Education Best Book of the Year and is the recipient of the Carter G. Woodson Book Award. Ms. Bolden is a two-time NAACP Image Award nominee and winner of the 2016 Children's Book Guild of Washington, DC's Nonfiction Award for Body of Work.